Dear Reader,

This book comes to you with easy-to-follow, nutritious recipes that are inspired by Mediterranean classics and other one pot dishes with some clever twists. The recipes were designed for **busy cooks** who multitask and sometimes run out of time. When this happens, we often end up ordering in or picking up takeout.

All the recipes incorporate the "one pot" approach to cooking a meal. Some methods are suited for a quickly prepared meal; others take a more slow-cooked approach.

I've compiled recipes focused on the Mediterranean diet that do not take much hands-on time but still result in a **delicious, wholesome meal** your family and friends will enjoy. Some of the methods employ basic cookware (sheet pans, baking dishes, and skillets), and others use appliances like a pressure cooker, Instant Pot®, or slow cooker.

One pot cooking has been around for generations, which is why I became interested in gathering these recipes for you. For years, I've enjoyed one pot dishes that my mother and grandmother made, some in a baking dish, others in a roasting pan, Dutch oven, or skillet. They both made many **memorable meals** in a pressure cooker. I've carried on the tradition in my own kitchen. I am sure you'll enjoy these dishes as much as I do.

Happy Cooking!

Peter Minaki

Welcome to the Everything® Series!

These handy, accessible books give you all you need to tackle a difficult project, gain a new hobby, comprehend a fascinating topic, prepare for an exam, or even brush up on something you learned back in school but have since forgotten.

You can choose to read an Everything® book from cover to cover or just pick out the information you want from our four useful boxes: Questions, Facts, Alerts, and Essentials. We give you everything you need to know on the subject, but throw in a lot of fun stuff along the way too.

question	fact
Answers to common questions.	Important snippets of information.

alert	essential
Urgent warnings.	Quick handy tips.

We now have more than 600 Everything® books in print, spanning such wide-ranging categories as cooking, health, parenting, personal finance, wedding planning, word puzzles, and so much more. When you're done reading them all, you can finally say you know Everything®!

PUBLISHER Karen Cooper

MANAGING EDITOR Lisa Laing

ASSOCIATE COPY DIRECTOR Casey Ebert

PRODUCTION EDITOR Jo-Anne Duhamel

ACQUISITIONS EDITOR Lisa Laing

DEVELOPMENT EDITOR Lisa Laing

EVERYTHING® SERIES COVER DESIGNER Erin Alexander

THE
EVERYTHING®
ONE POT
MEDITERRANEAN
COOKBOOK

PETER MINAKI

200 FRESH AND SIMPLE RECIPES THAT COME TOGETHER IN ONE POT

ADAMS MEDIA

NEW YORK   LONDON   TORONTO   SYDNEY   NEW DELHI

This book is dedicated to the hardworking, multitasking people out there trying to put a meal on the table in what sometimes feels like a shrinking day.

Acknowledgments

My sincere thanks to Lisa Laing of Simon & Schuster for her patience and encouragement during the writing process. Thank you to my friends, my father, and my brother and his family for allowing me to serve many of the dishes that appear in this book. Their feedback was valuable in developing the recipes.

Aadamsmedia

Adams Media
An Imprint of Simon & Schuster, Inc.
100 Technology Center Drive
Stoughton, Massachusetts 02072

An Everything® Series Book.

Everything® and everything.com® are registered trademarks of Simon & Schuster, Inc.

First Adams Media trade paperback edition April 2023

ADAMS MEDIA and colophon are trademarks of Simon & Schuster.

For information about special discounts for bulk purchases, please contact Simon & Schuster Special Sales at 1-866-506-1949 or business@simonandschuster.com.

The Simon & Schuster Speakers Bureau can bring authors to your live event. For more information or to book an event, contact the Simon & Schuster Speakers Bureau at 1-866-248-3049 or visit our website at www.simonspeakers.com.

Interior design by Kellie Emery
Interior photographs by James Stefiuk
Nutritional analysis by Linn Steward, RDN

Manufactured in the United States of America

10 9 8 7 6 5 4 3 2

Library of Congress Cataloging-in-Publication Data has been applied for.

ISBN 978-1-5072-2023-8
ISBN 978-1-5072-2024-5 (ebook)

Contains material adapted from the following titles published by Adams Media, an Imprint of Simon & Schuster, Inc.: *The Everything® Green Mediterranean Cookbook* by Peter Minaki, copyright © 2021, ISBN 978-1-5072-1662-0; *The Everything® Healthy Mediterranean Cookbook* by Peter Minaki, copyright © 2019, ISBN 978-1-5072-1150-2; and *The Everything® Mediterranean Instant Pot® Cookbook* by Kelly Jaggers, copyright © 2020, ISBN 978-1-5072-1250-9.

Contents

CHAPTER 5: SLOW COOKER DISHES   131

Introduction

The Mediterranean region is known for its beauty, diversity, variety of seafood, and the diet that takes its name from the area surrounding the Mediterranean Sea. Despite the many countries that make up the Mediterranean region, the Mediterranean diet is most commonly associated with Spain, Southern France, Italy, Greece, and the Middle East. There are regional differences in what constitutes the Mediterranean diet, but the essential common feature is a focus on whole grains, fruits, vegetables, and fish. Meat is part of the Mediterranean diet, but it is considered a treat or served as part of a celebration or seasonal customs, such as Christmas, feast days, or Easter.

Traditionally, family gatherings in this region were centered around the kitchen table. Families were large, and households typically included grandparents along with parents and children. Preparing a meal for the family had to be an efficient, time-sensitive, and structured process so that a busy cook had time to multitask as a meal was cooking. One pot meals were (and still are) common: Large pots of soup or stew would sit on an open fire or on a wood-burning stove. Deep roasting pans were filled with seasonal vegetables along with fish or meat and placed in a wood-burning oven. Baked pasta dinners in large casserole dishes bubbled in the oven and sent out tantalizing aromas. Everything needed for a meal was in that single cooking vessel.

While households are smaller now, the appeal of one pot cooking is still strong. We continue to look for satisfying meals that are put together easily and need little hands-on attention. And it's always good to reduce the number of pans that need to be washed! You probably already have most of the equipment needed to make the recipes in this book: baking sheets, skillets, roasting pans, and a stockpot. A slow cooker is the ultimate "set-it-and-forget-it" appliance. Fill it early in the day, turn it on, and dinner is ready when you are. Meals that once took hours to make can be ready in a fraction of the time when you use a pressure cooker or Instant Pot®.

Mediterranean cuisine focuses on food that is in season. People cook what they find at their local farmers' market. Vegetables such as eggplants and peppers are consumed in the summer months, while cabbage and cauliflower are enjoyed in the winter. When preparing the recipes in this book, try to use local ingredients that are in season. You can create authentic Mediterranean dishes by buying local seasonal ingredients and by stocking your pantry with some specialty items that are central to Mediterranean cooking, such as Greek sheep's or goat's milk feta, tomato passata, or tahini. Most of the specialty items mentioned in these recipes can be found at Greek or Middle Eastern grocers, but many supermarkets carry these items too. Just look for them in the international product aisles.

Whether you're looking for a quickly sautéed skillet supper, a hearty and warming stew, or a complete dinner with all the ingredients roasted side by side on one sheet pan, you'll find plenty of options. Try Fettucine with Mushroom Bolognese (Chapter 2) on a busy weeknight, or roast a pan of Greek Meatballs with Roast Potatoes (Chapter 3) for an impressive but easy Sunday lunch. For pasta night, make Skillet Lasagna (Chapter 2), Sheet Pan Gnocchi and Shrimp (Chapter 3), or Pasta Shells Stuffed with Roasted Red Peppers and Feta (Chapter 7). Of course, you'll want some ideas for desserts, and Chapter 8 has plenty. Some of them don't need a pan at all! Stuffed Figs take a few minutes to assemble, but they make a sophisticated dessert that your guests won't soon forget. And once you taste the intense citrus flavor of the Sicilian Whole Orange Cake, you'll want to make it over and over.

No matter which recipe you choose, take a cue from the people of the Mediterranean region—relax and savor your meal and the company of others. Taking time to smell, taste, and appreciate the flavors of a meal improves the feelings of satisfaction and enjoyment. The one pot approach to cooking allows you to have more time to spend with those important people in your life while enjoying a tasty and satisfying meal. Healthy eating has never been more delicious—or easy!

CHAPTER 1

The Flavors of the Mediterranean— All in One Pot

While there may be as many Mediterranean diets as there are countries in the Mediterranean, all of the diets from the region have one thing in common: They build meals around plant foods and most often prepare them in their whole form. Vegetables, fruits, legumes, whole grains, and healthy fats take center stage, while animal products serve as supporting players. Research indicates that the people in these regions have the lowest rates of chronic diseases and among the highest life expectancies in the world. A key aspect of the Mediterranean diet is a lifestyle that values moderation in every aspect, including the level of everyday stress. With this cookbook, you'll be able to relieve the stress associated with planning and cooking healthy meals regularly. Making one pot meals, whether on the stovetop, in the oven, or using a convenient countertop appliance, means you'll spend less time cooking and cleaning and more time savoring your meals and enjoying the company of the people you eat them with.

What's So Special about the Mediterranean Diet?

Studies show that in comparison to consumers of the traditional Western diet, the people of the Mediterranean live longer, weigh less, and suffer from fewer medical complaints, such as cardiovascular disease. Researchers looked at their lifestyles and found that the key to their abundant good health was their diet, their activity level, and the amount of time they spent with friends and family. They don't count calories, they don't deprive themselves, and they don't believe in bland meals.

What does all this mean? The Mediterranean diet is a heart-healthy eating plan that focuses on fresh, plant-based meals, healthy fats, and whole grains. Meals are made up of vegetables, whole grains, legumes, pulses (beans, lentils, and peas), pasta, fresh fruit, nuts, and rice. Healthy fats (such as olive oil) replace other fats (such as butter), dairy products are eaten in moderation, and fresh herbs and spices are used more than salt. Seafood is enjoyed occasionally—roughly two or three servings of fish or other seafood a week—while poultry is eaten about once a week, and red meat is limited to one to two servings a month.

Even without restricting the amount of food you eat, consuming the foods of the Mediterranean can help you to lose weight. Combining the diet with a reduction in your daily calorie intake makes weight loss even more likely.

The Mediterranean diet encourages lifestyle changes in addition to dietary changes, like incorporating more physical activity into your day. Go for a long walk before or after dinner, participate in sports, or take the stairs at work instead of the elevator. Adding more movement into your daily routine will improve your health and your mood.

> **fact**
>
> A Nurses' Health Study (*Annals of Internal Medicine*, 2013) followed more than ten thousand women and found that those who adhered to a Mediterranean eating plan were 46 percent more likely to reach age seventy without chronic diseases like type 2 diabetes, kidney disease, lung disease, Parkinson's disease, and cancer—and without major declines in cognitive and physical function. The women who aged healthfully consumed more plant-based foods, whole grains, and fish; fewer processed and red meats; and a moderate amount of alcohol.

Another way to enhance your mood and enjoy your meals is to slow down and relish the occasions when you eat with friends and family. Spend time talking, pausing while you eat to enjoy the company of those around you. Finally, drink more water. The Mediterranean diet encourages staying hydrated with water or unsweetened drinks like coffee or tea. Sugary drinks, like juice or sodas, should be avoided. These changes may seem small, but they can have a big impact on your health over time.

Stocking a Mediterranean Kitchen

Mediterranean food is flavorful and simple to prepare. Having a well-stocked pantry will make planning and preparing a Mediterranean meal even easier. Here are some items you should always have on hand so that you are ready to cook many different Mediterranean meals.

Olive Oil

Extra-virgin olive oil is a staple of Mediterranean cooking. Most countries surrounding the Mediterranean Sea produce their own olive oil. Ripe olives are pressed, and the oil is filtered and then bottled or canned for consumer use.

Olive oil is used in cooking, baking, and dressings, and for frying. The smoke point for olive oil is 410°F, which is well above the ideal frying temperature of 365°F–375°F, so go ahead and fry with olive oil! Spend some time trying out different kinds to discover which ones you like the most. A good-quality olive oil can make a simple dish outstanding.

Spices and Herbs

Mediterranean cuisine uses a variety of herbs and spices. The recipes in this book feature common Mediterranean herbs such as parsley, dill, rosemary, thyme, sage, mint, fennel fronds, bay leaf, tarragon, and oregano.

Whenever possible, it's best to use herbs in their fresh state. However, oregano is more pungent in its dried state and goes wonderfully with Mediterranean ingredients, so feel free to use dried oregano if you don't have fresh leaves.

Spices add warmth to many dishes. Some common Mediterranean spices to keep on hand include cinnamon, cloves, allspice, nutmeg, anise, saffron, crushed red pepper flakes, and mastiha. Mastiha is a spice that comes from the island of Chios, Greece, in the Eastern Mediterranean. Mastiha is harvested from the sap of the local *Pistacia lentiscus* tree at specific times of the year. It has a unique woody, slightly piney, incense-like flavor. It is traditionally used in Christmas and Easter breads and desserts, but you can use it in savory dishes as well. Buy spices in small amounts, as they tend to get stale when stored for too long.

essential

To incorporate more fresh, less-processed foods into your diet, try the following tip: Make a grocery list once a week that always includes fresh foods that have long shelf lives. These foods include apples, oranges, onions, and winter squashes. All are readily available and inexpensive, and most people like them.

Dairy Products

Most of the cheese in the Mediterranean region is made from sheep's or goat's milk. These cheeses are easier to digest and have a more complex texture and flavor than the cheeses made from cow's milk that are common in North America. For example, a true feta cheese is made only in Greece, and it is made from sheep's or goat's milk or a blend of the two. Buy feta made in Greece; otherwise, it is not true feta.

Other Greek cheeses referenced in this book are kefalotyri, which is a sharp sheep's milk cheese; graviera, which is similar to a Gruyère; and kasseri, which is a mild table cheese. Halloumi is a wonderful cheese from Cyprus that holds up well on a grill. Romano, Parmesan, and ricotta are all familiar cheeses from the Mediterranean region.

Greek yogurt is a thick, flavorful yogurt that can be eaten on its own, with fruit, or in recipes as a healthier alternative to sour cream.

> **alert**
>
> All foods from animal sources (meat, fish, eggs, and dairy products) are to be eaten sparingly if one hopes to achieve the benefits of this healthful lifestyle.

Beans and Lentils

The Mediterranean diet is one of the most healthful in the world because it includes a large amount of beans and legumes. Most beans and lentils you purchase in the store are dried, meaning they will keep for a long time in your pantry. Make sure you have plenty of white beans, lima beans, lentils, and chickpeas. Dried beans and some lentils require soaking overnight before they can be used, so having canned beans on hand is good for those days when you're in a hurry. Chickpeas and navy beans are good choices.

Whole Grains

Whole grains figure prominently in Mediterranean cooking, and grocers know this. Whole grains like barley and farro have become familiar and are included on many shopping lists. Buy your favorite whole grains and store them in a cool, dry place.

Stocks

A good stock will elevate any dish. Making your own stock lets you choose which flavors to add and, most important, how much salt to add. Keep your freezer well "stocked" with quart-sized containers of vegetable stock.

Tomatoes, Potatoes, and Citrus Fruits

Although tomatoes, potatoes, lemons, and oranges are more recent additions to the Mediterranean pantry, it is hard to imagine cooking Mediterranean dishes without them. Buy tomatoes when they are in season. If you must use them in the winter, cherry tomatoes are a good choice. Always have cans of tomato paste and plum tomatoes on hand. They are great for flavoring sauces, soups, and stews.

Citrus fruits are widely available all year, but you can also use preserved lemons, a great pantry staple. Potatoes vary in color, texture, and size. Experiment with different kinds, and discover your favorites.

Olives

Have a variety of green and black olives in your pantry. They are wonderful for garnishing salads, making dips, or just eating as a snack.

Vinegars, Honey, and Molasses

Balsamic, red wine, white wine, and cider vinegars are a must in a Mediterranean pantry. They are used to flavor stews, soups, salads, and even desserts. Honey has been a part of Mediterranean cooking for centuries, and it continues to be an essential ingredient in both sweet and savory dishes. You will also find sweeteners such as pomegranate molasses and grape molasses in desserts and in dressings for salads.

One Pot Cooking 101

One benefit of one pot cooking is fewer pots, pans, and utensils to wash. You can add to this advantage by keeping parchment paper, aluminum foil, and nonstick cooking spray on hand. Use nonstick pans whenever feasible to reduce the time you spend scrubbing after meals.

In these pages, you'll find a broad range of recipes using a variety of techniques. There's something for everyone here—whether you're a novice cook looking to get a meal on the table in the fewest number of steps possible or are more experienced in the kitchen and want to add some mostly hands-off recipes to your weeknight repertoire. A one pot meal can be a simple dinner all roasted together on a sheet pan or a richly flavored, long-simmered stew made in a Dutch oven or a slow cooker. If you have an Instant Pot® or a pressure cooker, you can reduce cooking time by 50 percent or more. And skillet dinners need just a little prep work and some hands-on time at the stove for a complete and satisfying meal. One pot meals are flexible and forgiving, which allows you to substitute some ingredients to suit your taste or switch out something according to the season.

Skillet Basics

Skillets have a wide base, which means a lot of surface area for sautéing or browning. A long handle makes a skillet easy to hold on the stovetop. Most of the recipes in this cookbook serve four or more, so you'll need at least a 10" or 12" skillet. One of each is even better. You should also own a lid to fit your skillet. Glass lids let you see inside while a dish is cooking, so you can tell if the contents are in danger of burning or need more liquid. You can use a cast iron skillet, a stainless steel skillet, or a nonstick skillet. Having one of each gives you flexibility as you cook different recipes. Nonstick skillets make cleanup easier. Cast iron and stainless steel pans have heat-proof handles so they can go into the oven or under the broiler. Skillets are your best bet when you want to get a meal on the dinner table in as little as 30 minutes!

Sheet Pan Basics

The large, flat surface of a sheet pan or baking sheet gives you plenty of room to roast a protein and vegetables together without crowding. Sheet pans come in several sizes, but the two most common sizes for home cooks are quarter-sheet pans (13" × 9") and half-sheet pans (18" × 13"). A sturdy aluminum half-sheet pan with a 1" rim will work well with most of the recipes in this book. A sheet of parchment paper will keep ingredients from sticking to the pan when roasting; if you're broiling on the sheet pan, use aluminum foil instead. (Parchment paper may burn at temperatures of 500°F and above.) Cooking an entire meal on a parchment-lined baking sheet means you'll have practically no cleanup at all!

A roasting pan can be used for recipes that need to be cooked in a vessel with slightly higher sides.

Dutch Oven Basics

A Dutch oven is a heavy 5- or 6-quart pot made of heavy-duty cast iron, usually enamel coated. This versatile pot has two handles and a heavy lid that forms a tight seal. It can be used on a stovetop or in the oven. Its large, flat base allows you to sauté vegetables or brown meats first, then add more ingredients, reduce the heat, and simmer for long, slow cooking. The cast iron pot holds a steady heat while simmering on the stove or in the oven.

Properly maintained, a Dutch oven can last a lifetime. Never use a scouring pad on an enamel-coated Dutch oven and always wipe it dry after washing. Sometimes knicks and cracks can occur over time, and water can cause rust if the Dutch oven is not dried properly. For stovetop cooking, a stockpot or large covered saucepan can stand in for a Dutch oven.

Slow Cooker Basics

A slow cooker is one of the easiest options for making dinner. You add the ingredients, turn the slow cooker to high or low, and come back several hours later to a fully cooked meal. In its most basic form, a slow cooker is made up of a base with a heating element, the stoneware vessel that goes into the base, and a glass lid. The most common size holds 5 or 6 quarts.

> **alert**
>
> Resist the urge to check on the contents of your slow cooker. Every time you lift the lid, you let out some of the heat that has been slowly building up. Uncovering the slow cooker can add up to 30 minutes to the total cook time. So don't give in to temptation!

Slow cookers have three settings: low, high, and warm. The maximum temperature for both low and high settings is 215°F—each setting reaches that temperature at a different rate. For easier cleaning, spray the inside of the vessel with cooking spray before adding ingredients. Slow cookers are perfect for feeding a crowd with almost no effort.

Pressure Cooker Basics

Cooking food under high pressure brings the temperature above the boiling point and seals in moisture so that food cooks in a fraction of the usual time. You may own a stovetop or electric pressure cooker, but you're more likely to own a multi-cooker, like an Instant Pot®. These extremely popular appliances make pressure cooking easy and safe. Whether you have a pressure cooker or an Instant Pot®, you have the ability to sauté or brown foods in the same appliance. Here are a few general guidelines:

- Always cook with liquid (water or stock) and never fill the pot more than ⅔ full.
- Don't use frozen meat or vegetables in a pressure cooker.
- Use the pressure cooker's valve to safely release pressure before opening or wait for the pressure to naturally release.
- Be sure to read the manufacturer's directions before using a pressure cooker or Instant Pot® for the first time.

Baking Dish Basics

A baking or casserole dish is an oven-safe square, rectangular, or oval vessel that is usually made of glass, porcelain, or stoneware. The most common baking dish size is 13" × 9", but some are smaller or larger. Be sure to use a baking dish that "just fits" the food you are cooking to ensure it cooks according to the recipe. The deep walls of a baking dish make it easy to build layers, as in a lasagna. The surface area at the top allows for browning of the top layer, either in the oven or under a broiler, which adds a depth of flavor.

Baking pans are best used for baked goods because they allow for a delicate, even browning. They're also best for broiling, since a ceramic or glass dish may shatter under the high heat of the broiler. Baking dishes are used for casseroles, egg dishes, and fruit desserts like crisps and cobblers.

Try to avoid sudden temperature changes when using a baking dish. Taking a preassembled baking dish from the refrigerating and placing it directly in a hot oven may cause it to crack. And when you remove a hot dish from the oven, place it on a wire rack to cool for a few minutes before serving.

CHAPTER 2

Skillet Dishes

Mushroom Fricassee

THE LIFE SPAN OF A MUSHROOM

The most common mushrooms you'll see in the grocery store are white (or "button"), cremini, and portobello mushrooms. Did you know that these are all the same type of mushroom, picked at different times? Button mushrooms are picked earliest, while they're still white. As they grow, the mushrooms turn brown and are called creminis. Finally, the mushrooms grow in size to become the giant portobellos. The mushrooms lose water as they mature, so the darker and larger ones are the most flavorful.

This dish is popular in Southern France on the Mediterranean Sea. The food of this region is more similar to that of Italy or Greece than of Paris.

2 tablespoons extra-virgin olive oil

8 ounces white mushrooms, halved

1 cup diced yellow onion

3 cloves garlic, peeled and minced

½ cup diced carrot

10 ounces baby spinach

1½ cups vegetable stock

1 tablespoon lemon juice

1 teaspoon salt

½ teaspoon ground black pepper

1 teaspoon cornstarch

4 teaspoons cold water

½ cup finely chopped fresh parsley

½ cup finely chopped fresh dill

1 Heat oil in a large skillet over medium-high heat. Sauté mushrooms for 5–6 minutes until browned. Add onion, garlic, and carrot and reduce heat to medium. Sauté for 5–6 minutes until softened.

2 Add spinach and stir for 1–2 minutes until wilted.

3 Stir in stock, lemon juice, salt, and pepper. Cover and cook for 20 minutes. Uncover and cook another 5 minutes.

4 In a small bowl, mix cornstarch and water. Stir mixture into skillet and cook for 1–2 minutes until sauce thickens.

5 Top with parsley and dill and serve.

Strapatsatha

Strapatsatha is a dish brought to Greece by the Sephardic Jews from Spain. It's a kind of omelet with fresh tomatoes and feta. There are many variations of this classic dish.

1 tablespoon extra-virgin olive oil

6 ounces chorizo sausage, sliced

4 large ripe tomatoes, grated

½ cup diced sweet banana pepper

3 scallions, trimmed and sliced

1 cup crumbled feta cheese

8 large eggs, beaten

½ teaspoon ground black pepper

SERVES 6	
Per Serving:	
Calories	339
Fat	25g
Sodium	683mg
Carbohydrates	8g
Fiber	2g
Sugar	5g
Protein	20g

1 Heat oil in a large skillet over medium-high heat. Add sausage and sauté for 2 minutes. With a slotted spoon, remove sausage from the skillet and set aside. Take skillet off heat and let cool for 5 minutes.

2 Return skillet to medium heat and add tomatoes. Cook for 5 minutes or until most of liquid is evaporated. Add banana pepper and scallions and cook for 2 more minutes. Add cheese and cook for 1 minute.

3 Add eggs, black pepper, and cooked sausage. Carefully stir egg mixture as it cooks until just set. Serve hot or at room temperature.

Chickpeas with Leeks and Spinach

SERVES 4

Per Serving:

Calories	351
Fat	11g
Sodium	1,237mg
Carbohydrates	52g
Fiber	14g
Sugar	14g
Protein	14g

Slightly sweet and richly flavored, balsamic vinegar isn't just for salads. It adds a unique flavor to this vegetarian stew.

2 tablespoons extra-virgin olive oil

2 cups sliced leeks

3 cloves garlic, peeled and minced

4 cups drained and rinsed canned chickpeas

2 bay leaves

2 cups tomato sauce

1 cup finely chopped fresh parsley

2 tablespoons balsamic vinegar

½ teaspoon salt

½ teaspoon ground black pepper

4 cups baby spinach

¼ cup chopped fresh mint

1 Heat oil in a large skillet over medium-high heat. Sauté leeks and garlic for 5 minutes. Stir in chickpeas, bay leaves, tomato sauce, parsley, vinegar, salt, and pepper. Add enough hot water to just cover contents. Bring to a boil.

2 Reduce heat to low, cover, and simmer for 30 minutes. Remove from heat.

3 Remove and discard bay leaves.

4 Stir in spinach and mint. Serve immediately.

Eggs in Italian Bread

SERVES 6

Per Serving:	
Calories	371
Fat	9g
Sodium	1,233mg
Carbohydrates	54g
Fiber	3g
Sugar	7g
Protein	17g

Use the best crusty bread you can find for this classic Italian breakfast.

6 (2") slices crusty Italian bread

3 teaspoons olive oil, divided

2 medium red bell peppers, seeded and thinly sliced

1 small shallot, peeled and minced

6 large eggs

½ teaspoon salt

½ teaspoon ground black pepper

1 Using a cookie cutter or glass, cut out large circles from the center of each bread slice. Discard center pieces and set hollowed-out bread slices aside.

2 Heat 1 teaspoon oil in a large skillet over medium heat. Sauté bell peppers and shallot for 5–7 minutes or until tender. Remove from skillet and drain on paper towels; keep warm.

3 Add remaining 2 teaspoons oil to skillet over medium-high heat. Place bread slices in pan. Crack one egg into hollowed-out center of each bread slice. Cook for 5 minutes, then flip carefully and cook for 3 minutes more. Transfer to plates and top with bell pepper mixture.

4 Season with salt and black pepper before serving.

Leek and Prune Stew

This combination of prunes and leeks is a nice balance of sweet and savory. Serve it with crusty whole-grain bread.

2 tablespoons extra-virgin olive oil

3 cups chopped leeks

16 pitted prunes

1 cup tomato purée

2 bay leaves

½ teaspoon salt

¼ teaspoon ground black pepper

2 tablespoons balsamic vinegar

SERVES 4	
Per Serving:	
Calories	199
Fat	7g
Sodium	307mg
Carbohydrates	35g
Fiber	4g
Sugar	18g
Protein	2g

1 Heat oil in a large, high-sided skillet over medium-high heat. Add leeks and sauté for 6–7 minutes until translucent.

2 Add prunes, tomato purée, bay leaves, salt, pepper, and just enough hot water to cover. Bring to a boil.

3 Reduce heat to low, cover, and simmer for 30 minutes. Uncover and simmer for 5 minutes.

4 Remove and discard bay leaves. Stir in vinegar before serving.

DRIED FRUITS

Dried fruits such as figs, raisins, dates, apricots, and plums (prunes) have been part of the Mediterranean diet for centuries. Drying fruit is one of the oldest forms of preservation and is still popular today.

Mushroom Giouvetsi

SERVES 6

Per Serving:

Calories	221
Fat	1g
Sodium	1,016mg
Carbohydrates	44g
Fiber	5g
Sugar	8g
Protein	8g

SAVE TIME!

Buy sliced mushrooms instead of slicing them yourself. Most stores carry several varieties in the produce section. Cremini and button are popular small mushrooms. Portobello mushrooms are large and meaty.

Mushrooms do a great job of replacing meat in recipes. For more flavor, top Mushroom Giouvetsi with grated Pecorino Romano cheese.

½ cup dried mushrooms (any type)

6 cups hot vegetable stock

2 tablespoons extra-virgin olive oil

1 large yellow onion, peeled and diced

1 medium carrot, peeled and grated

1 stalk celery, trimmed and finely diced

2 cups sliced fresh button mushrooms

2 cloves garlic, peeled and minced

¼ cup dry white wine

2 cups crushed tomatoes

2 bay leaves

1 teaspoon fresh thyme leaves

1 teaspoon dried oregano

½ teaspoon salt

½ teaspoon ground black pepper

1 cup orzo

½ teaspoon ground nutmeg

¼ cup chopped fresh parsley

1 Place dried mushrooms in a large bowl and cover with stock. Set aside to soak for 10 minutes. Drain mushrooms, reserving stock. Roughly chop mushrooms and set aside.

2 Heat oil in a large skillet over medium-high heat. Sauté onion, carrot, celery, and fresh mushrooms for 5–7 minutes until softened. Add garlic and sauté for 1 minute. Add wine, tomatoes, bay leaves, thyme, oregano, salt, and pepper. Bring to a boil. Reduce heat to medium-low and simmer for 25–30 minutes until most of the liquid has cooked down. Remove and discard bay leaves.

3 Increase heat to high and add orzo to the skillet. Cook, stirring, for 5 minutes. Add chopped mushrooms and reserved stock. Bring to a boil, then reduce heat to medium-low. Simmer for 8 minutes, stirring occasionally. Allow to cool for 5 minutes. Sprinkle with nutmeg and parsley before serving.

Skillet Fettucine Alfredo

This recipe uses a smaller amount of cream than most fettucine Alfredo recipes. Milk is the main dairy ingredient, with just ¼ cup of cream added at the end for richness. The starch in the pasta helps thicken the sauce.

2 tablespoons unsalted butter

½ cup grated yellow onion

1 clove garlic, peeled and minced

2 cups hot chicken stock

1½ cups whole milk

1 pound fettucine

¼ cup heavy cream

½ cup grated Parmesan cheese

1 teaspoon sea salt

¼ teaspoon ground black pepper

⅛ teaspoon ground nutmeg

¼ cup finely chopped fresh parsley

1 Melt butter in a large, high-sided skillet over medium heat. Sauté onion and garlic for 3 minutes.
2 Add stock, milk, and pasta and bring to a boil over high heat. Reduce heat to medium-low and simmer for 18 minutes (add more milk if the mixture seems too thick).
3 Stir in cream, cheese, salt, pepper, and nutmeg. Top with parsley before serving.

SERVES 4

Per Serving:

Calories	652
Fat	20g
Sodium	1,597mg
Carbohydrates	93g
Fiber	6g
Sugar	8g
Protein	24g

Fettucine with Mushroom Bolognese

Mushrooms are great on their own, but in this recipe they are on double duty, acting as a meat substitute. Many supermarkets now sell a variety of sliced mushrooms, so you can experiment with different flavors and textures.

¼ cup dried porcini mushrooms

2 cups hot water

3 tablespoons extra-virgin olive oil

1 large yellow onion, peeled and diced

4 cloves garlic, peeled and minced

1 large carrot, peeled and grated

1 stalk celery, trimmed and finely diced

1½ cups chopped cremini mushrooms

1½ cups chopped oyster mushrooms

1 teaspoon sea salt

½ teaspoon ground black pepper

½ cup dry white wine

½ teaspoon ground nutmeg

3 bay leaves

2 cups crushed tomatoes

1 teaspoon fresh thyme leaves

1 teaspoon dried Greek oregano

1 pound fettucine, cooked

2 tablespoons chopped fresh parsley

½ cup grated Parmesan cheese

1 Place porcini mushrooms in a small bowl and cover with water. Set aside for 10 minutes. Strain and chop mushrooms. Set aside.

2 Heat oil in a large skillet over medium-high heat. Sauté onion, garlic, carrot, celery, and cremini and oyster mushrooms for 8 minutes. Season with salt and pepper and reduce heat to medium-low. Simmer for 5 minutes or until almost all the liquid has cooked down.

3 Stir in rehydrated porcini mushrooms, wine, nutmeg, and bay leaves. Simmer until liquid is reduced by half, about 15 minutes.

4 Add tomatoes and thyme. Increase heat to medium-high and bring to a boil. Reduce heat to low and simmer until sauce is thick, about 30 minutes. Stir in oregano and remove and discard bay leaves.

5 Add pasta and toss to coat well. Top with parsley and cheese and serve.

Caramelized Onion Pasta

This dish is about contrasts: The sweet caramelized onions play against the tart and creamy yogurt. Use full-fat yogurt and allow it to come to room temperature before adding.

1/4 cup unsalted butter

2 large yellow onions, peeled, halved, and sliced

1 tablespoon sugar

2 tablespoons balsamic vinegar

1 cup plain whole-milk Greek yogurt

1 cup hot water

1 pound bucatini, cooked

1/4 cup grated dry mizithra cheese

1/4 cup chopped fresh chives

SERVES 4

Per Serving:

Calories	404
Fat	17g
Sodium	262mg
Carbohydrates	47g
Fiber	3g
Sugar	9g
Protein	15g

1 Melt butter in a large skillet over medium-high heat. Add onions and sugar and cook, stirring occasionally, until very soft, about 10 minutes. Reduce heat to medium-low, cover, and cook for 15–20 minutes, stirring occasionally.

2 Uncover and add vinegar. Simmer uncovered for 5–10 minutes or until most of the liquid is gone and onions are brown and tender. Remove from heat.

3 Stir in yogurt and water, then add pasta and stir to combine.

4 Top with cheese and chives before serving.

Sfougato

MAKE IT YOUR OWN

Think of sfougato as a building block dish. Try it with different vegetables, herbs, or cheeses. It's a great way to use up what's in your refrigerator. You can even toss in leftover roast potatoes or fries. Use your imagination, but use seasonal ingredients for best results.

For Greeks, eggs are not limited to breakfast. This omelet often makes an appearance at the lunch or dinner table as an appetizer or a main course.

1 medium yellow onion, peeled and finely diced

4 tablespoons all-purpose flour

¼ cup dried bread crumbs

2 tablespoons finely chopped fresh mint

½ cup crumbled feta cheese

½ teaspoon salt

½ teaspoon ground black pepper

1 tablespoon dried thyme

8 large eggs

2 tablespoons extra-virgin olive oil

1 Preheat oven to 350°F.
2 Combine onion, flour, bread crumbs, mint, cheese, salt, pepper, and thyme in a medium bowl; mix well.
3 In a large bowl, add eggs and beat well. Stir in onion mixture.
4 Add oil to a large oven-safe skillet over medium-high heat. When oil is hot, add egg mixture. Cook for 4–5 minutes or until thickened, stirring constantly. Flip omelet, reduce heat to medium, and cook another 4–5 minutes until eggs are set.
5 Transfer skillet to oven and bake 5 minutes. Serve immediately.

Bianko from Corfu

This dish comes from the Ionian island of Corfu. Although the island is Greek, its most popular dishes have an Italian flair.

3 tablespoons extra-virgin olive oil, divided

2 large yellow onions, peeled and sliced

6 cloves garlic, peeled and minced

2 medium carrots, peeled and sliced

1 cup chopped celery

½ teaspoon salt

1 teaspoon ground black pepper

4 large russet potatoes, peeled and cut into ½" slices

4 (5-ounce) whitefish fillets (cod or grouper), skinned

4 tablespoons lemon juice

¼ cup chopped fresh parsley

1 Heat 1 tablespoon oil in a large, high-sided skillet over medium heat. Add onions, garlic, carrots, and celery. Cook for 5–7 minutes or until onions soften. Season with salt and pepper.

2 Add potatoes and just enough hot water to cover. Increase heat to medium-high and bring to a boil. Reduce heat to medium-low, cover the skillet, leaving the lid slightly ajar, and cook for 12 minutes.

3 Place fillets over potatoes and top with remaining 2 tablespoons oil. Cover and cook for another 12–15 minutes or until fish is opaque and flaky.

4 Uncover skillet and add lemon juice. Don't stir it; shake skillet back and forth to allow liquid to penetrate the layers.

5 Place fish and potatoes on a large platter and top with parsley. Serve immediately.

SERVES 4

Per Serving:

Calories	628
Fat	19g
Sodium	434mg
Carbohydrates	78g
Fiber	11g
Sugar	8g
Protein	37g

WHITEFISH

Whitefish has a light, flaky white flesh. Low in fat, whitefish is a healthful meal option. Halibut, cod, sea bass, pollock, tilapia, and hake are all considered whitefish.

Cod with Mussels

Mussels are a good sustainable seafood choice. They're not only a good source of protein; they actually filter carbon out of their environment.

4 (4-ounce) cod fillets

1 teaspoon sea salt

½ teaspoon ground black pepper

⅓ cup bread crumbs

3 teaspoons minced garlic, divided

½ cup chopped fresh parsley

¼ cup plus 1 tablespoon chopped fresh dill, divided

3 tablespoons olive oil, divided

1 pound mussels, scrubbed and beards removed

¼ cup dry white wine

1 medium yellow onion, peeled and minced

1 small red Calabrian chili, seeded and minced

1 tablespoon Dijon mustard

½ medium red bell pepper, seeded and thinly sliced

1 tablespoon cornstarch

2 tablespoons cold water

1 teaspoon dried Greek oregano

1½ teaspoons lemon juice

2 medium zucchini, trimmed and sliced into thin ribbons

SERVES 4

Per Serving:

Calories	320
Fat	13g
Sodium	922mg
Carbohydrates	19g
Fiber	3g
Sugar	5g
Protein	28g

CLEANING MUSSELS

Before you use them, mussels need a good cleaning and sorting. Rinse and scrub the mussels. Tap any mussels that are opened. If they don't close, discard them. Pull the beards from the mussels and rinse. Use them right away or refrigerate for up to 1 day.

1 Place fillets on a flat surface. Season with salt and black pepper. In a small bowl, combine bread crumbs, 1 teaspoon garlic, parsley, and ¼ cup dill. Top each fillet with bread crumb mixture.

2 Heat 1 tablespoon oil in a large skillet over high heat. Add mussels and wine. Cover and steam for 5 minutes or until shells open. Transfer to a colander set over a bowl to catch the broth. Remove meat from half the mussels and leave the other half intact. Set aside.

3 In the same skillet, heat remaining 2 tablespoons oil over medium heat. Sauté onion and chili for 5 minutes. Add remaining 2 teaspoons garlic and sauté 1 minute. Stir in mustard and reserved mussel broth. Bring to a gentle boil. Add fillets and bell pepper to the skillet, reduce heat to low, cover, and cook for 12 minutes.

4 In a small bowl, stir cornstarch with water until smooth. Add to skillet and stir. Remove from heat and add mussels, oregano, and remaining 1 tablespoon dill. Drizzle with lemon juice.

5 Divide zucchini ribbons among four plates. Top each with a fillet, mussels, and sauce. Serve immediately.

Cod with Raisins

SERVES 4

Per Serving:

Calories	317
Fat	8g
Sodium	100mg
Carbohydrates	30g
Fiber	2g
Sugar	21g
Protein	32g

In ancient Greece, raisins were often used as a seasoning in savory dishes. They add a sweet taste to this unusual meal.

2 tablespoons extra-virgin olive oil

2 medium yellow onions, peeled and chopped

1 tablespoon tomato paste diluted in ¾ cup water

¾ cup raisins

1 cup water

1½ pounds cod

1 Heat oil in a large skillet over medium heat. Add onions and sauté for 5 minutes, stirring constantly. Add tomato paste and simmer for 10 minutes. Stir in raisins and continue to cook for 3 more minutes.

2 Add water and increase heat to high. Bring to a boil, then reduce heat to medium-low and simmer for 30 minutes until raisins are plump. Add cod and simmer for 15 minutes until sauce has thickened. Serve immediately.

Lentils with Fish

Use your favorite whitefish fillets for this satisfying dish. If using frozen fillets, thaw them in the refrigerator overnight.

1 pound dried green or brown lentils, drained and rinsed

3 tablespoons extra-virgin olive oil, divided

1 medium yellow onion, peeled and diced

1 medium carrot, peeled and diced

½ cup diced red bell pepper

2 bay leaves

3 cloves garlic, peeled and minced

½ cup tomato sauce

2 cups vegetable broth

4 (5-ounce) cod, haddock, or catfish fillets

1 teaspoon sea salt

¾ teaspoon ground black pepper

½ teaspoon sweet paprika

1 teaspoon red wine vinegar

2 teaspoons dried oregano

4 teaspoons capers

SERVES 4

Per Serving:

Calories	648
Fat	13g
Sodium	1,218mg
Carbohydrates	81g
Fiber	14g
Sugar	7g
Protein	55g

1 Place lentils in a large skillet with just enough water to cover and bring to a boil over high heat. Immediately remove from heat, drain, and rinse with cold water. Set aside.

2 In the same skillet, heat 2 tablespoons oil over medium-high heat. Add onion, carrot, bell pepper, bay leaves, and garlic and cook for 5 minutes or until softened. Add lentils and stir to coat. Add tomato sauce and broth and bring to a boil. Reduce heat to low, cover, and simmer for 45 minutes or until most of the liquid has been absorbed.

3 Brush both sides of fish with remaining 1 tablespoon oil and sprinkle with salt, black pepper, and paprika. Place fillets over lentils. Cover and cook for 8–10 minutes until fish turns opaque.

4 Remove and discard bay leaves. Drizzle with vinegar and sprinkle oregano and capers over the top. Serve immediately.

Pan-Fried Sole with Asparagus

SERVES 2

Per Serving:

Calories	361
Fat	26g
Sodium	372mg
Carbohydrates	5g
Fiber	2g
Sugar	2g
Protein	28g

This is a flexible and quick meal. If asparagus isn't available, use the same technique with broccolini or green beans.

2 (6-ounce) sole or haddock fillets

½ teaspoon sea salt

¼ teaspoon ground black pepper

2 tablespoons olive oil

2 tablespoons unsalted butter, softened

3 tablespoons lemon juice

6 spears asparagus, trimmed

½ cup minced fresh parsley

1 Pat fillets dry with a paper towel and season with salt and pepper.
2 Heat oil in a large skillet over medium-high heat. Carefully place fillets in pan. Cook for 2 minutes per side. Transfer fillets to a plate and keep warm.
3 Reduce heat to medium and melt butter. Add lemon juice and cook for 30 seconds. Add asparagus to pan and simmer for 2 minutes until bright green and tender-crisp. Return fillets to pan and simmer for 1–2 minutes until warmed through.
4 Sprinkle with parsley and serve immediately.

Bay Scallops with Lemon Spaghetti

Bay scallops are small, about the size of your fingertip. They are sweet, cook quickly, and are more affordable than their larger diver scallop cousins.

3 tablespoons extra-virgin olive oil, divided

1 pound bay scallops

1 medium yellow onion, peeled and finely chopped

3 cloves garlic, peeled and minced

2 tablespoons minced fresh ginger

½ cup dry white wine

1 cup heavy cream

½ teaspoon sea salt

¼ teaspoon ground black pepper

12 ounces spaghetti, cooked, with 1 cup cooking water reserved

1 teaspoon grated lemon zest

1½ teaspoons lemon juice

½ cup minced fresh chives

1 Heat 2 tablespoons oil in a large skillet over medium heat. Sauté scallops for 3 minutes. Remove scallops from skillet and set aside.

2 Add remaining 1 tablespoon oil to skillet. Sauté onion, garlic, and ginger for 6–7 minutes until onion is translucent.

3 Stir in wine and simmer for 5 minutes. Add cream, salt, and pepper and simmer for 3 minutes.

4 Add pasta, scallops, lemon zest, lemon juice, and reserved pasta water. Toss to incorporate and cook for 3 minutes or until scallops are firm and opaque.

5 Top with chives and serve.

SERVES 4

Per Serving:

Calories	549
Fat	33g
Sodium	867mg
Carbohydrates	56g
Fiber	2g
Sugar	4g
Protein	21g

CREAMINESS WITHOUT CREAM

If you want to avoid using cream in the sauce, replace it with more pasta water. Or you can stir in some whole-milk Greek yogurt instead. Just make sure to remove the skillet from the heat when you do.

Seared Scallops with Green Peas and Pancetta

Pancetta is an Italian salt-cured pork product made from the belly. It is Italy's version of bacon and is used to enhance many dishes.

12 large sea scallops, brought to room temperature

1 teaspoon sea salt, divided

¾ teaspoon coarsely ground black pepper, divided

4 tablespoons extra-virgin olive oil, divided

1 cup diced pancetta

¾ cup water, divided

¼ cup finely diced yellow onion

2 cups fresh or frozen green peas

¼ cup dry white wine

2 teaspoons fresh thyme leaves

1 tablespoon lemon juice

1 Pat scallops dry with a paper towel and season with ½ teaspoon each salt and pepper.

2 Heat 2 tablespoons oil in a large nonstick skillet over medium-high heat. Sear scallops for 2 minutes per side. Transfer to a plate and set aside.

3 Place pancetta and ½ cup water in skillet over medium heat. Cook for 6–7 minutes until fat is rendered, water evaporates, and pancetta crisps in the fat. Remove with a slotted spoon and transfer to a paper towel–lined plate. Pour off excess fat.

4 Add 1 tablespoon oil to skillet over medium heat. Stir in onion and remaining ¼ cup water. Use a wooden spoon to deglaze by scraping up any browned bits from the bottom of the skillet. Add peas, wine, thyme, remaining ½ teaspoon salt, and remaining ¼ teaspoon pepper. Cook, stirring occasionally, for 3–5 minutes until most of the liquid has cooked down.

5 Stir in pancetta. Nestle scallops in the pea and pancetta mixture. Cook for 2 minutes or until scallops are opaque.

6 Drizzle with lemon juice and remaining 1 tablespoon oil. Serve immediately.

Shrimp Saganaki

Saganaki *refers to the two-handled cooking vessel traditionally used to serve this appetizer. A heavy skillet works just as well. You'll need lots of crusty bread for this dish.*

2 tablespoons extra-virgin olive oil

½ cup sliced button mushrooms

¼ cup finely chopped red onion

¼ cup diced green bell pepper

¼ cup diced red bell pepper

1 medium tomato, diced

½ cup crumbled feta cheese

1 teaspoon dried oregano

¼ teaspoon crushed red pepper flakes

1 ounce ouzo

¼ teaspoon salt

8 extra-large shrimp, peeled and deveined

¼ cup grated mozzarella cheese

SERVES 2	
Per Serving:	
Calories	344
Fat	25g
Sodium	908mg
Carbohydrates	10g
Fiber	2g
Sugar	6g
Protein	14g

1 Heat oil in a large oven-safe skillet over medium-high heat. Add mushrooms and sauté for 2–3 minutes or until browned. Add onion, bell peppers, and tomato.

2 Reduce heat to medium and simmer for 5–7 minutes.

3 Preheat broiler.

4 Remove skillet from heat and stir in feta, oregano, pepper flakes, ouzo, and salt. Add shrimp, nestling them slightly into the sauce. Top with mozzarella.

5 Broil for 5–6 minutes until shrimp are pink and cheese is golden brown.

Greco Linguine with Shrimp

Although Italians avoid pairing seafood and cheese, Greeks enjoy the contrast of tangy feta with briny, sweet shrimp. It's easy to tell when shrimp are done. They turn pink and curl into a C shape. Overcooked shrimp tighten into the form of an O.

Per Serving:

Calories	406
Fat	20g
Sodium	837mg
Carbohydrates	42g
Fiber	4g
Sugar	3g
Protein	14g

A "GOOD" FAT

Olive oil is a monounsaturated fat that has been shown to raise HDL levels ("good" cholesterol) in blood.

3 tablespoons extra-virgin olive oil, divided

3 cloves garlic, peeled and sliced

1 pint cherry tomatoes, halved

½ cup halved, pitted Kalamata olives

1 tablespoon dried Greek oregano

1 medium zucchini, trimmed, halved lengthwise, and cut into half-moon slices

24 medium shrimp, peeled and deveined

1 teaspoon balsamic vinegar

1 pound linguine, cooked and still hot

¼ cup crumbled feta cheese

1 cup chopped fresh parsley

1 Heat 2 tablespoons oil in a large skillet over medium-high heat. Sauté garlic for 1 minute, then stir in tomatoes, olives, and oregano. Bring to a boil. Reduce heat to medium-low and simmer for 10 minutes.

2 Stir in zucchini, shrimp, and vinegar. Cook, stirring constantly, until shrimp turn pink, about 5 minutes.

3 Remove from heat and add pasta, cheese, and parsley and toss to coat pasta.

4 Drizzle with remaining 1 tablespoon oil and serve immediately.

Risotto with Shrimp, Mushrooms, and Asparagus

This rich and creamy risotto is an entire meal in a bowl! And it's pretty enough for a company dinner. Drizzle each serving with some good-quality olive oil for extra Mediterranean flavor.

2 tablespoons olive oil, divided

1 pound large shrimp, peeled and deveined

1 teaspoon sea salt

½ teaspoon ground black pepper

1 medium yellow onion, peeled and finely diced

3 cloves garlic, peeled and minced

1¼ cups Arborio rice

1 pound button mushrooms, sliced

2 bay leaves

1 teaspoon dried thyme

¼ cup dry white wine

3 cups hot seafood or vegetable stock

12 spears asparagus, trimmed and cut into 1" pieces

1 teaspoon grated lemon zest

SERVES 4

Per Serving:

Calories	211
Fat	8g
Sodium	1,724mg
Carbohydrates	13g
Fiber	2g
Sugar	5g
Protein	20g

1. Heat 1 tablespoon oil in a large skillet over medium-high heat. Add shrimp in a single layer and season with salt and pepper. Sauté until shrimp just turns pink, about 1 minute per side. Remove shrimp with a slotted spoon and set aside on a paper towel–lined plate.

2. Add remaining 1 tablespoon oil to skillet. Sauté onion and garlic for 5 minutes.

3. Add rice and stir to coat and toast for 2 minutes. Add mushrooms, bay leaves, thyme, and wine and cook, stirring constantly, until wine is completely absorbed.

4. Reduce heat to medium and add stock a ladle at a time, stirring constantly until each ladle is absorbed. Continue stirring and adding stock until stock is used up and rice is tender. This should take about 20 minutes.

5. Remove and discard bay leaves. Stir in asparagus, lemon zest, and shrimp. Cook for 2 minutes to warm asparagus and shrimp.

6. Serve immediately.

Aegean Shrimp with Pearl Couscous

SERVES 4

Per Serving:

Calories	408
Fat	14g
Sodium	1,495mg
Carbohydrates	40g
Fiber	3g
Sugar	3g
Protein	26g

Pearl couscous is also called Israeli couscous. It's a toasted pasta in the shape of small beads. Tender and satisfying, pearl couscous makes a delicious substitute for rice.

2 tablespoons extra-virgin olive oil, divided

1 pound large shrimp, peeled and deveined

1 teaspoon sea salt

½ cup finely diced yellow onion

2 tablespoons tomato paste

1 cup pearl couscous

2 cups hot water

1 ounce ouzo

¼ teaspoon crushed red pepper flakes

¾ cup crumbled feta cheese

½ cup finely chopped fresh parsley

1 Heat 1 tablespoon oil in a large skillet over medium-high heat. Add shrimp in a single layer and sprinkle with salt. Sauté for 1 minute per side. Transfer shrimp to a plate.

2 Reduce heat to medium and add remaining 1 tablespoon oil. Sauté onion for 5 minutes.

3 Add tomato paste, couscous, water, ouzo, and pepper flakes. Cover and cook for 5 minutes.

4 Uncover skillet and stir in shrimp.

5 Top with cheese and parsley before serving.

Chicken Fricassee

Many fantastic dishes also come from the South of France, like this Chicken Fricassee. This one pan meal combines chicken, mushrooms, and baby spinach.

3 tablespoons olive oil, divided

4 (4-ounce) chicken legs

4 (6-ounce) bone-in chicken thighs

2 teaspoons sea salt

½ teaspoon ground black pepper

8 pearl onions, peeled

3 cups halved button mushrooms

1 cup diced yellow onion

3 cloves garlic, peeled and minced

4 tablespoons all-purpose flour

½ cup dry white wine

1 cup warm whole milk

3 cups hot chicken stock

3 bay leaves

4 sprigs fresh thyme

3 cups baby spinach

½ chopped fresh parsley

SERVES 4

Per Serving:	
Calories	574
Fat	33g
Sodium	1,984mg
Carbohydrates	20g
Fiber	2g
Sugar	7g
Protein	44g

FRICASSEE

Fricassee is a thick French stew of meat in a white sauce. It's most often made with chicken, but other meats, like veal or pork, can be used. Mushrooms are traditionally included, but you can improvise with whatever vegetables you have on hand.

1 Heat 2 tablespoons oil in a large skillet over medium-high heat. Season chicken on both sides with salt and pepper. Cook until browned, about 3 minutes per side. Transfer to a platter.

2 Add pearl onions to pan and sauté for 5–6 minutes until browned on all sides. Transfer to platter with chicken.

3 Add remaining 1 tablespoon oil and sauté mushrooms for 2 minutes. Add yellow onion and garlic and reduce heat to medium. Sauté for 4–5 minutes or until onion is just translucent. Stir in flour and cook for 1 minute. Add wine and use a wooden spoon to scrape up browned bits from the bottom of the pan.

4 Add milk, stock, bay leaves, thyme, chicken pieces (skin side up), pearl onions, and spinach and bring to a low boil. Partially cover skillet and reduce heat to low. Simmer for 30 minutes, then uncover and simmer for another 10 minutes or until sauce has thickened.

5 Remove and discard bay leaves and thyme sprigs. Garnish with parsley before serving.

Skillet Chicken Parmesan

SERVES 4

Per Serving:

Calories	583
Fat	32g
Sodium	937mg
Carbohydrates	19g
Fiber	2g
Sugar	3g
Protein	51g

This crowd-pleasing weeknight meal is easy to prepare in one skillet. Serve it with a green salad.

⅔ cup cornmeal

⅓ cup all-purpose flour

1 teaspoon dried oregano

1 teaspoon minced fresh basil

1 teaspoon minced fresh rosemary

4 (6-ounce) boneless, skinless chicken breasts

5 tablespoons olive oil, divided

¾ teaspoon salt, divided

½ teaspoon ground black pepper, divided

1 medium yellow onion, peeled and diced

6 cloves garlic, peeled and minced

3 cups canned whole tomatoes, hand crushed

¼ cup dry white wine

1 cup roughly chopped fresh basil

2 cups grated mozzarella cheese

1 In a large bowl, combine cornmeal, flour, oregano, minced basil, and rosemary. Set aside.

2 Place chicken on a flat surface and cover with plastic wrap. Using a heavy pot or kitchen mallet, pound chicken to ½" thickness. Cut chicken pieces in half. Brush pieces with 2 tablespoons oil and season with ½ teaspoon salt and ¼ teaspoon pepper. Dredge chicken in reserved cornmeal and flour mixture.

3 Heat 2 tablespoons oil in a large skillet over medium-high heat. Add chicken (in batches) and fry for 2–3 minutes per side or until browned. Place chicken on a large paper towel–lined tray to soak up excess oil. Discard oil used for frying and wipe skillet clean.

4 Heat remaining 1 tablespoon oil in skillet over medium heat. Add onion and garlic and cook for 5–6 minutes. Add tomatoes and wine. Increase heat to medium-high and bring to a boil, then reduce heat to medium-low. Season with remaining ¼ teaspoon each salt and pepper. Nestle chicken into sauce. Cover and cook for 30 minutes until sauce thickens and chicken is tender.

5 Top with chopped basil and cheese. Cover skillet for 2 minutes to let cheese melt. Serve warm.

Chicken Thighs with Scallions

READY RICE

Having a supply of cooked rice on hand makes weekday meal prep easier. Make a large batch of white or brown rice at the beginning of the week and store in sealed containers in the refrigerator. You can reheat rice in the microwave, but it's even better when heated slowly in a saucepan over medium heat. Stir in a tablespoon of water as the rice heats.

Boneless, skinless chicken thighs are as simple to prepare as boneless breasts, but they're much more flavorful.

4 bunches scallions, trimmed

8 (3-ounce) boneless, skinless chicken thighs

1 teaspoon sea salt

1 teaspoon ground black pepper

¼ cup all-purpose flour

2 tablespoons olive oil

½ cup dry white wine

1½ cups chicken broth

1 bay leaf

2 teaspoons fresh thyme leaves

¼ cup heavy cream

4 sprigs fresh thyme

1 Cut scallions into two pieces, separating the white sections from the green parts. Chop scallion greens. Set aside.

2 Place chicken on a large sheet of plastic wrap and cover with another sheet. Use a mallet or small heavy saucepan to pound chicken to a uniform thickness. Season with salt and pepper.

3 Place flour in a shallow bowl. Dredge chicken in flour and set on a wire rack.

4 Heat oil in a large nonstick skillet over medium heat. Sear chicken in hot oil for 2 minutes per side. Arrange white sections of scallions around chicken and cook on both sides until golden, about 3 minutes. Add wine and cook for 2 minutes. Stir in broth, bay leaf, and thyme leaves. Bring to a gentle boil, then reduce heat to low. Simmer uncovered for 15 minutes.

5 Add cream and continue to simmer until sauce has thickened enough to coat the back of a wooden spoon, about 4 minutes. Remove and discard bay leaf. Stir in scallion greens.

6 Spoon some cream sauce onto each of four plates and then lay a row of scallion whites on top, followed by 2 chicken thighs. Garnish with thyme sprigs and serve.

Chicken Cacciatore

Chicken Cacciatore is chicken prepared "hunter's style." This means it's cooked in a tomato-based sauce with onions, bell peppers, and mushrooms. It makes a wonderful Sunday dinner.

1/2 cup all-purpose flour

1 (3-pound) whole chicken, cut into pieces

1 teaspoon salt

1/2 teaspoon ground black pepper

1/4 cup extra-virgin olive oil

1 (3-ounce) Italian turkey sausage, casings removed

2 medium yellow onions, peeled and diced

1 large carrot, peeled and chopped

1 stalk celery, trimmed and chopped

1/3 cup diced green bell pepper

1 cup sliced cremini mushrooms

3 bay leaves

2 teaspoons chopped fresh rosemary

1 tablespoon tomato paste

1/4 cup chopped fresh parsley

4 cloves garlic, peeled and minced

1 cup dry white wine

1 (28-ounce) can plum tomatoes, hand crushed

1/2 cup low-sodium chicken broth

SERVES 6

Per Serving:

Calories	374
Fat	16g
Sodium	563mg
Carbohydrates	17g
Fiber	2g
Sugar	4g
Protein	33g

WHOLE CHICKEN

Buying a whole chicken and segmenting it yourself is the most economical choice. But this recipe can be made with bone-in thighs, drumsticks, or breast halves.

1 Place flour in a shallow bowl. Season chicken pieces with salt and black pepper and dredge in flour. Heat oil in a deep skillet over medium-high heat. Add chicken and brown for 5 minutes per side. Remove from pan and set aside.

2 Add sausage to pan and cook, breaking it up with a wooden spoon, for 3 minutes. Add onions, carrot, celery, bell pepper, mushrooms, bay leaves, and rosemary. Sauté for 7 minutes until onions are translucent. Stir in tomato paste, parsley, garlic, and wine. Cook, stirring occasionally, for 5 minutes until liquid is reduced by one-third.

3 Return chicken pieces, plus any accumulated juices, to the pan. Add plum tomatoes and broth and bring to a boil. Reduce heat to low, partially cover pan, and simmer for 60–80 minutes until sauce is thickened and chunky.

4 Remove and discard bay leaves. Serve hot.

Pumpkin Risotto with Pancetta

*Using canned pumpkin makes this recipe an easy weeknight meal.
You can use fresh pumpkin or squash if you like. Simmer cubes
of pumpkin or squash in water or stock for 20–25 minutes until
fork-tender, then drain and mash.*

1 cup diced pancetta

¼ cup water

2 tablespoons extra-virgin olive oil

1 cup diced yellow onion

2 cloves garlic, peeled and minced

1½ cups Arborio rice

½ cup dry white wine

5 cups hot vegetable or chicken stock

1½ cups canned pumpkin purée

½ cup grated Parmesan or Romano cheese

2 tablespoons unsalted butter

1 teaspoon sea salt

¼ teaspoon ground black pepper

1 tablespoon thyme leaves

SERVES 4	
Per Serving:	
Calories	584
Fat	28g
Sodium	2,185mg
Carbohydrates	60g
Fiber	5g
Sugar	7g
Protein	15g

1 Place pancetta and water in a large skillet over medium heat.
   Cook for 6–7 minutes until fat is rendered, water evaporates, and
   pancetta crisps in the fat. Remove with a slotted spoon and transfer to a paper towel–lined plate. Pour off excess fat, leaving about
   1 tablespoon

2 Add oil, onion, and garlic and sauté for 5 minutes. Add rice and
   cook, stirring often, for 2 minutes. Add wine and continue stirring
   until almost all wine has been absorbed, about 5 minutes.

3 Add stock a ladle at a time, stirring constantly until each ladle is
   absorbed. Continue stirring and adding stock until stock is used
   up and rice is tender. This should take about 20 minutes.

4 Stir in pumpkin, cheese, butter, and half of the pancetta. Season
   with salt and pepper.

5 Divide risotto among four shallow bowls and top each with thyme
   and remaining pancetta. Serve immediately.

Pork with Leeks and Halloumi Cheese

Per Serving:

Calories	461
Fat	33g
Sodium	711mg
Carbohydrates	6g
Fiber	1g
Sugar	2g
Protein	31g

HALLOUMI

Halloumi is a firm, brined Cypriot cheese that is traditionally made with sheep's or goat's milk, or sometimes a combination of the two. You can find cow's milk halloumi, but it's worthwhile to search for the real thing from Cyprus. It has a high melting point, so it can handle searing and grilling without falling apart.

Cubes of firm, flavorful halloumi make a surprisingly good alternative to potatoes in this satisfying dish. Don't skip the drizzle of lemon juice at the end. It adds a bright counterpoint to the richness of the pork and cheese.

4 tablespoons extra-virgin olive oil, divided

10 ounces halloumi cheese, cubed

1½ pounds boneless pork shoulder, cut into 1" cubes

1½ teaspoons sea salt

1 teaspoon ground black pepper

½ cup dry white wine

½ cup chicken stock

2 medium leeks, trimmed and sliced

1 tablespoon lemon juice

1 tablespoon dried Greek oregano

1 teaspoon crushed red pepper flakes

1 Heat 2 tablespoons oil in a large skillet over medium heat. Brown cheese cubes in hot oil until golden on all sides, 7–8 minutes. Transfer cheese to a paper towel–lined plate and set aside.

2 Season pork with salt and black pepper.

3 Add half the pork to skillet and brown on all sides for 5–6 minutes. Transfer to a paper towel–lined plate. Add 1 tablespoon oil to skillet and repeat with remaining pork cubes.

4 Add wine, stock, and leeks to skillet. Use a wooden spoon to deglaze by scraping up the browned bits off the bottom of the skillet. Return pork to skillet. Increase heat to medium-high and bring just to a boil.

5 Reduce heat to medium-low, cover, and simmer for 20 minutes or until leeks are lightly browned and pork is fork-tender.

6 Remove from heat and stir in cheese cubes. Drizzle with lemon juice and remaining 1 tablespoon oil. Sprinkle with oregano and pepper flakes and serve.

Italian Sausage and Zucchini

Choose hot or sweet sausage, depending on your taste. Chicken or turkey sausages are also an option—they're usually available in a variety of flavors.

1 pound Italian sausage, casings removed

1 cup diced yellow onion

3 cloves garlic, peeled and minced

1/4 cup dry white wine

2 large zucchini, trimmed, halved lengthwise, and cut into 1/2" slices

1 (28-ounce) can whole tomatoes, hand crushed

1 teaspoon minced fresh rosemary

1 teaspoon dried oregano

1 teaspoon sea salt

1/4 teaspoon ground black pepper

2 bay leaves

1 pound penne rigate, cooked

1/4 cup grated Parmesan cheese

SERVES 4

Per Serving:

Calories	489
Fat	19g
Sodium	1,488mg
Carbohydrates	54g
Fiber	7g
Sugar	11g
Protein	24g

1 Roll sausage meat into 1" meatballs.

2 Heat a large skillet over medium-high heat. Cook meatballs until browned on all sides, 7–8 minutes. Reduce heat to medium and add onion and garlic. Sauté for 4–5 minutes or until onion is translucent.

3 Add wine and cook for 1 minute. Stir in zucchini, tomatoes, rosemary, oregano, salt, pepper, and bay leaves. Cook uncovered for 12–15 minutes until sauce has thickened. Remove and discard bay leaves.

4 Stir in pasta and top with cheese.

5 Serve immediately.

Skillet Lasagna

SERVES 6

Per Serving:

Calories	516
Fat	20g
Sodium	1,606mg
Carbohydrates	57g
Fiber	5g
Sugar	10g
Protein	25g

CHOOSE YOUR SAUSAGE

You'll see lots of options for Italian sausage at the store. Some are fennel flavored, some are spicy, and some are made from turkey or chicken. Experiment with different varieties to find your favorite.

Lasagna doesn't have to be just for weekends anymore. This skillet version comes together in less than an hour.

1 pound mild Italian sausage, casings removed

1 cup diced yellow onion

3 cloves garlic, peeled and minced

2 bay leaves

½ cup dry white wine

3 cups tomato sauce

1 cup beef stock

½ cup whole milk

1 teaspoon sea salt

½ teaspoon ground black pepper

12 ounces no-boil lasagna noodles

1 teaspoon dried oregano

¼ cup chopped fresh basil

½ cup whole-milk ricotta cheese

1 cup shredded mozzarella cheese

¼ cup grated Parmesan cheese

1 Place sausages in a large skillet over medium-high heat and cook, breaking them up with a wooden spoon, until browned, 4–5 minutes. Add onion, garlic, bay leaves, and wine and cook, stirring for 3 minutes. Stir in tomato sauce, stock, milk, salt, and pepper.

2 Break lasagna noodles into smaller pieces and press the pieces into the sauce. Add hot water if needed to just cover noodles.

3 Cover, reduce heat to medium-low, and simmer for 15–18 minutes, stirring occasionally, until pasta is tender and sauce is thick.

4 Remove and discard bay leaves. Stir in oregano and basil. Top with ricotta and mozzarella, cover skillet, and reduce heat to low. Cook for 3–4 minutes until cheese melts.

5 Top with Parmesan and serve.

Spetsofai

This is a one pan dish of spicy sausages, onions, peppers, and tomatoes. Pick your favorite sausage and enjoy this spetsofai with crusty bread and a dry red wine.

3 tablespoons extra-virgin olive oil, divided

4 (3-ounce) hot Italian sausages

4 medium-sized hot banana peppers, seeded and skins pierced

2 large red or yellow bell peppers, seeded and sliced

2 medium yellow onions, peeled and sliced

4 cloves garlic, peeled and minced

2 large ripe tomatoes, peeled and grated

½ teaspoon salt

½ teaspoon ground black pepper

2 teaspoons dried oregano

SERVES 8	
Per Serving:	
Calories	161
Fat	11g
Sodium	315mg
Carbohydrates	10g
Fiber	3g
Sugar	5g
Protein	6g

1 Heat 2 tablespoons oil in a large skillet over medium-high heat. Add sausages and brown for 2–3 minutes on each side. Remove sausages from skillet and set aside.

2 Add banana peppers to skillet and fry on all sides until just brown, 1–1½ minutes per side. Remove from pan and slice. Set aside.

3 Add bell peppers, onions, garlic, and tomatoes. Bring mixture to a boil and then reduce heat to medium-low. Season with salt and black pepper. Slice sausages. Add sausages and banana peppers to skillet. Cover and cook for 15–20 minutes or until sauce thickens.

4 Uncover skillet and add oregano. Drizzle remaining 1 tablespoon oil over sausage mixture. Serve hot.

Pasta Shells with Sausage, Arugula, and Cream Sauce

THE PERFECT SHAPE

Pasta shells are great for holding sauce in their "cups." But you can use other short pasta shapes, like ziti, rigatoni, or farfalle.

This method of cooking the pasta and the sauce in the same skillet is a game changer. You save time and save on washing an extra pot.

3 (3-ounce) Italian sausages, casings removed
1 tablespoon olive oil
1 medium yellow onion, peeled and diced
2 cloves garlic, peeled and minced
4 sun-dried tomatoes in oil, drained and sliced
1 teaspoon sea salt
¼ teaspoon ground black pepper
½ cup dry white wine
8 ounces small pasta shells
2 cups heavy cream
2 cups hot water
½ teaspoon ground fennel seeds
6 cups arugula or baby spinach
¼ cup chopped fresh chives
½ cup grated Parmesan cheese
¼ teaspoon crushed red pepper flakes

1 Place sausages in a large, high-sided skillet over medium-high heat and cook, breaking them up with a wooden spoon, until browned, 4–5 minutes.

2 Reduce heat to medium and add oil, onion, garlic, tomatoes, salt, and black pepper. Cook for 5 minutes, then stir in wine and cook for 2 minutes more.

3 Add pasta, cream, water, and fennel seeds. Increase heat to medium-high and bring to a boil. Reduce heat to low and simmer for 6 minutes, stirring occasionally.

4 Add arugula in batches and stir in until just wilted. Stir in chives and cheese and sprinkle with pepper flakes.

5 Serve immediately.

Beef Noodles with Brandy and Mushrooms

Beef, brandy, and mushrooms are a happy trio in this sophisticated weeknight dinner. Splurge on a rib eye cut for the most tender morsels of brandy-flavored beef.

MAKE YOUR OWN DRIED TOMATOES

Making "sun-dried" tomatoes in your kitchen is incredibly simple. Simply slice plum tomatoes in half lengthwise and season with salt and pepper. Bake them in a 200°F oven for 3 hours and voilà! For a fraction of the cost, you can indulge in the wonderful, sweet flavor of dried tomatoes. Toss them with olive oil before serving on pasta or bread. Leftovers can be frozen for up to 3 months.

4 tablespoons olive oil, divided

2 pounds boneless veal or rib eye steak, cut into bite-sized pieces

1½ teaspoons sea salt, divided

1 teaspoon ground black pepper

2 cups sliced cremini or button mushrooms

1 cup diced yellow onion

2 cloves garlic, peeled and minced

⅓ cup sliced sun-dried tomatoes

3 bay leaves

4 sprigs fresh thyme

¼ cup brandy

2 cups beef stock

½ cup white wine

1 pound pappardelle or tagliatelle, cooked

4 tablespoons unsalted butter

⅓ cup chopped fresh parsley

1 Heat 2 tablespoons oil in a large, deep skillet over high heat.

2 Season meat with 1 teaspoon salt and ½ teaspoon pepper and place in hot skillet. Sauté for 6–7 minutes until browned. Remove from skillet and set aside.

3 Add remaining 2 tablespoons oil to pan and reduce heat to medium. Sauté mushrooms, onion, and garlic for 5 minutes. Return meat to skillet, along with sun-dried tomatoes, bay leaves, thyme, brandy, stock, wine, and remaining ½ teaspoon each salt and pepper. Bring to a boil, then reduce heat to medium-low. Cover and simmer for 5 minutes.

4 Add pasta and toss to mix. Cover and simmer for 5 minutes or until sauce has thickened.

5 Remove from heat and stir in butter. Remove and discard bay leaves and thyme sprigs. Top with parsley and serve.

CHAPTER 3

Sheet Pan and Roasting Pan Dishes

Roasted Carrots with Honey and Thyme

Per Serving:

Calories	232
Fat	18g
Sodium	376mg
Carbohydrates	16g
Fiber	4g
Sugar	10g
Protein	1g

ARISTAEUS

According to Greek mythology, a lesser god by the name of Aristaeus was credited with teaching humankind husbandry and agriculture, including the art of beekeeping for honey.

This recipe may just sway people who resist eating vegetables. The honey brings out the sweetness of the roasted carrots, while the thyme and wine keep the dish on the savory side. For a twist, try maple syrup instead of honey.

8 medium carrots, peeled
⅓ cup extra-virgin olive oil
1 teaspoon grated orange zest
1 tablespoon honey
2 tablespoons dry white wine
½ teaspoon salt
½ teaspoon ground black pepper
2 teaspoons fresh thyme leaves

1 Preheat oven to 400°F.
2 In a large bowl, combine carrots, oil, orange zest, honey, wine, salt, pepper, and thyme. Stir to coat. Empty contents of the bowl evenly onto a large baking sheet.
3 Bake 25–30 minutes or until tender. Serve immediately or at room temperature.

Baked Zucchini Patties

This recipe is popular in the summer months when gardens and local markets are teeming with zucchini. Baked Zucchini Patties pack well for a road trip or picnic.

3 medium zucchini, trimmed and grated

1½ teaspoons salt, divided

1 cup thinly sliced scallions

1 tablespoon onion powder

1 clove garlic, peeled and minced

1 large egg, lightly beaten

2 tablespoons chopped fresh mint or 1 tablespoon dried mint

1 tablespoon chopped fresh dill

1 tablespoon chopped fresh parsley

¼ cup plain bread crumbs

⅓ cup all-purpose flour

1 teaspoon baking powder

¼ cup grated graviera or Gouda cheese

½ cup crumbled feta cheese

½ teaspoon ground black pepper

2 tablespoons olive oil

SERVES 4

Per Serving:

Calories	240
Fat	14g
Sodium	1,271mg
Carbohydrates	20g
Fiber	3g
Sugar	5g
Protein	10g

PERFECT PATTIES

When using zucchini to make patties, it's important to draw out as much liquid as possible before mixing with the other ingredients. Don't skimp on the draining time and squeeze the grated zucchini as hard as you can to remove excess liquid. Your patties will be crisp on the outside and light and tender on the inside.

1 Place zucchini in a large colander set over a bowl. Sprinkle with 1 teaspoon salt, cover, and refrigerate at least 3 hours.

2 Preheat oven to 425°F. Line a large baking sheet with parchment paper and spray with nonstick cooking spray.

3 Place zucchini on a large kitchen towel, roll it up, and squeeze out as much liquid as you can. Transfer to a large bowl. Add scallions, onion powder, garlic, egg, mint, dill, parsley, bread crumbs, flour, baking powder, cheeses, pepper, and remaining ½ teaspoon salt. Stir until incorporated.

4 Form 2 tablespoons zucchini mixture into a ball and flatten into a small patty. Place on prepared baking sheet. Repeat with remaining mixture, spacing the patties about 1" apart. Brush patties with oil.

5 Bake on the lowest oven rack for 8 minutes. Flip patties and bake for another 8 minutes.

6 Serve warm.

Mediterranean Sheet Pan Vegetarian Dinner

For a nice twist, try this vegetarian crowd-pleaser with sweet potatoes. If you're feeling adventurous, crumble some feta on top when it comes out of the oven.

1½ pounds small new potatoes, halved

1 large carrot, peeled and chopped

1½ cups sliced yellow onion

2 cloves garlic, peeled and minced

1 (15-ounce) can chickpeas, drained and rinsed

1½ teaspoons grated lemon zest

4 sprigs fresh thyme

1 teaspoon dried Greek oregano

1 teaspoon sweet paprika

1 teaspoon sea salt

½ teaspoon ground black pepper

¼ cup extra-virgin olive oil

1 pound fresh green beans, trimmed

½ cup chopped fresh parsley

SERVES 4	
Per Serving:	
Calories	379
Fat	16g
Sodium	749mg
Carbohydrates	54g
Fiber	8g
Sugar	7g
Protein	9g

1 Preheat oven to 425°F and line a large baking sheet with parchment paper.

2 In a large bowl, combine potatoes, carrot, onion, garlic, chickpeas, lemon zest, thyme, oregano, paprika, salt, and pepper. Drizzle with oil and toss to coat. Transfer to prepared baking sheet.

3 Bake for 25 minutes. Remove baking sheet from oven and add green beans. Stir to combine and return to oven. Bake for 10 minutes.

4 Remove and discard thyme sprigs. Top with parsley and serve.

Broiled Eggplant

BROILER PANS

If you plan to do a lot of broiling, purchasing a broiler pan will be a good investment. Broiler pans work well because the vents and grooves in the rack allow the grease to drain off whatever foods are being cooked.

If you use small Chinese eggplants, cut them in half rather than into slices.

4 small eggplants, trimmed and sliced lengthwise into ⅛" pieces

4 cloves garlic, peeled and minced

1 tablespoon olive oil

¾ teaspoon salt, divided

½ teaspoon ground black pepper

1 Preheat broiler.
2 In a large bowl, toss eggplant slices with garlic, oil, ½ teaspoon salt, and pepper. Place eggplant slices on a broiler pan or large baking sheet.
3 Broil for 5 minutes per side until golden brown outside and soft inside. Season with remaining ¼ teaspoon salt.

Patates Plaki

This is a traditional Greek vegetarian dish featuring the potato as the star. With the other vegetables in the mix, a wonderful symphony of flavors comes together from the roasting process. Don't be afraid to drizzle more olive oil when the potatoes come out of the oven.

6 large Yukon Gold potatoes, peeled and quartered

3 cloves garlic, peeled and smashed

1 medium yellow onion, peeled and roughly chopped

½ medium red bell pepper, seeded and sliced

½ medium green bell pepper, seeded and sliced

½ medium carrot, peeled, halved lengthwise, and sliced

1 large ripe tomato, grated

2 bay leaves

1 teaspoon sweet paprika

1 teaspoon crushed red pepper flakes

1 teaspoon dried Greek oregano

1 cup chicken stock

2 teaspoons sea salt

1 teaspoon ground black pepper

⅓ cup extra-virgin olive oil

1 Preheat oven to 425°F.
2 Place potatoes, garlic, onion, bell peppers, carrot, tomato, bay leaves, paprika, pepper flakes, and oregano in a large roasting pan. Toss to coat. Stir in stock, salt, and black pepper.
3 Drizzle with oil and roast for 45–50 minutes until potato tops are crisp but there's still some sauce in the pan.
4 Allow to cool for 5 minutes. Remove and discard bay leaves before serving.

SERVES 8

Per Serving:

Calories	308
Fat	10g
Sodium	718mg
Carbohydrates	52g
Fiber	6g
Sugar	5g
Protein	6g

CRUSHED RED PEPPER

Crushed red pepper flakes are made from hot peppers that are dried and crushed. Most crushed red pepper flakes include the seeds, which are the hottest part of the pepper. Depending on the peppers used, some brands are hotter than others. Be careful when you first use them. Add only a little at a time to make sure the dish is not too hot for your taste. You can always add more heat, but you can't take it away.

Roast Sweet Potatoes with Feta

SERVES 4

Per Serving:

Calories	448
Fat	25g
Sodium	907mg
Carbohydrates	48g
Fiber	7g
Sugar	11g
Protein	9g

Although they have a sweet flavor, sweet potatoes are low on the glycemic scale. Salty, rich feta cheese makes a perfect companion.

2 pounds sweet potatoes, peeled and cut into 1" pieces

5 tablespoons extra-virgin olive oil, divided

¾ teaspoon sea salt

¼ teaspoon ground black pepper

¼ teaspoon ground cinnamon

1 cup crumbled feta cheese

½ cup sliced scallions

1 Preheat oven to 425°F. Line a large baking sheet with parchment paper.

2 Place sweet potatoes on prepared baking sheet. Drizzle with 4 tablespoons oil and sprinkle with salt, pepper, and cinnamon. Toss to coat.

3 Roast for 40 minutes, stirring once halfway through cooking time.

4 Top with cheese and scallions. Drizzle with remaining 1 tablespoon oil before serving.

Imam Bayildi

SERVES 12

Per Serving:

Calories	147
Fat	7g
Sodium	398mg
Carbohydrates	20g
Fiber	8g
Sugar	10g
Protein	3g

WHY DID THE IMAM FAINT?

The literal translation of *imam bayildi* is "the imam fainted." It's unclear why he fainted. Some say it's because the dish was so delicious that he was overcome. Others think he fainted at the cost of the dish. Either way, it is a swoon-worthy dish.

This lighter version of a much-loved Turkish/Greek dish uses much less olive oil than traditional recipes, but flavor is not compromised here. Eggplant is best in the summer months when it's in season. Otherwise, use Japanese eggplant.

6 medium eggplants, trimmed and cut in half lengthwise

6 tablespoons extra-virgin olive oil, divided

2 teaspoons sea salt

1 teaspoon ground black pepper

1 medium green bell pepper, seeded and sliced

10 cloves garlic, peeled and thinly sliced

2½ cups sliced yellow onion, divided

3 large Roma tomatoes, thinly sliced

2 teaspoons dried Greek oregano

½ cup chopped fresh parsley

1 Preheat oven to 400°F. Line a large baking sheet with parchment paper.

2 Place eggplant halves cut side up on a work surface. Use a sharp knife to score each half, making a crisscross pattern. Drizzle with 2 tablespoons oil and sprinkle with salt and black pepper. Place halves cut side down on prepared sheet. In one corner of the sheet, place bell pepper, garlic, and 2 cups onion. Drizzle with 2 tablespoons oil and toss to coat.

3 Bake for 30 minutes or until eggplant just begins to soften. Flip eggplant halves so they're cut side up.

4 Press into the center of each eggplant half with the underside of a ladle to form a shallow impression. Fill each half with the roasted pepper, garlic, and onion mixture. Top with tomatoes and remaining ½ cup sliced onions. Drizzle with remaining 2 tablespoons oil. Sprinkle with oregano and parsley.

5 Bake for 45–60 minutes until most of the liquid has cooked down and topping is golden brown.

6 Serve hot or at room temperature.

Baked Oysters with Tomatoes, Capers, and Feta

A fresh raw oyster topped with a squeeze of lemon is a great treat. But if you're trying oysters for the first time, baking them is a good introduction.

3 medium plum tomatoes, chopped

½ cup thinly sliced scallions

2 cloves garlic, peeled and sliced

2 teaspoons capers

2 tablespoons dry white wine

½ teaspoon smoked paprika

1 teaspoon fresh thyme leaves

¼ teaspoon crushed red pepper flakes

½ cup bread crumbs

1 cup crumbled feta cheese

12 fresh oysters, shucked and bottom shells reserved

1 large lemon, cut into wedges

1 Preheat oven to 450°F.
2 In a large bowl, combine tomatoes, scallions, garlic, capers, wine, paprika, thyme, and pepper flakes.
3 Stir in bread crumbs and cheese. Place oysters on a large baking sheet in their bottom shells. Divide topping mixture evenly over oysters.
4 Bake on middle rack for 15–20 minutes or until tops are golden brown. Serve oysters hot or warm with lemon wedges.

SERVES 4

Per Serving:	
Calories	207
Fat	10g
Sodium	520mg
Carbohydrates	19g
Fiber	2g
Sugar	6g
Protein	11g

CAPERS

Capers are flavorful unopened buds from the *Capparis spinosa* bush. They can be packed in salt or brine. Try to find the smallest ones—they seem to have more flavor than the big ones do. Capers are great on their own or incorporated into sauces. They are also good in salads and as a garnish on many dishes that would otherwise be dull.

Parchment Salmon

SALMON

Salmon is one of the most healthful fish and one of the tastiest. It helps with heart health, is high in protein, and is rich in omega-3 fatty acids.

Try this method with any type of fish. If you would like to use an oilier fish, such as bluefish, increase the onions and decrease the butter.

¼ cup unsalted butter, softened

½ pound button mushrooms, chopped

1 tablespoon minced shallot

½ cup chopped scallions

2 teaspoons chopped fresh marjoram

1½ pounds salmon fillet

¼ cup dry white wine

1 Combine butter, mushrooms, shallot, scallions, and marjoram in a small bowl.

2 Preheat oven to 400°F.

3 Cut salmon into four portions. Cut four pieces of parchment paper (about three times the size of each portion) and place them on a flat surface. Set a salmon piece in the middle of each sheet and top with 1 tablespoon butter mixture. Sprinkle with 1 tablespoon wine. For each packet, fold parchment over the top and continue to fold until sealed. Place packets on a large baking sheet.

4 Roast for 7–10 minutes until paper is slightly brown. Slit open paper and serve immediately.

Broiled Red Mullet with Garlic and Herbs

In the Mediterranean, red mullet is prized for its sweet, firm but flaky meat. If you can't find it, try red snapper or drum fillets as a good substitute.

2 tablespoons lemon juice

1½ teaspoons grated lemon zest

½ cup extra-virgin olive oil, divided

4 tablespoons chopped fresh parsley, divided

1 teaspoon fresh thyme leaves

¼ teaspoon ground black pepper

¾ teaspoon sea salt, divided

4 (1-pound) red mullets, scaled and gutted

1 clove garlic, peeled and minced

1 teaspoon dried Greek oregano

1 medium lemon, cut into wedges

1 Preheat broiler. Grease a large baking sheet.

2 In a medium bowl, whisk together lemon juice, lemon zest, ¼ cup oil, 2 tablespoons parsley, thyme, pepper, and ½ teaspoon salt.

3 Place fillets on prepared baking sheet and brush inside and outside of fillets with some of the lemon mixture.

4 Broil for 5 minutes. Flip fillets and brush with remaining lemon mixture. Broil for another 5 minutes.

5 In a small bowl, combine remaining ¼ cup oil, remaining 2 tablespoons parsley, and remaining ¼ teaspoon salt with garlic and oregano. Whisk together.

6 Drizzle garlic sauce over fish and serve immediately with lemon wedges.

SERVES 4

Per Serving:

Calories	455
Fat	34g
Sodium	557mg
Carbohydrates	1g
Fiber	0g
Sugar	0g
Protein	35g

HOW TO PICK THE FRESHEST FISH

Fresh fish should smell only of the sea. The eyes should be bright and shiny, not sunken. Open the gills with your finger; they should be bright red. Finally, press your finger into the body; the flesh should be firm and the scales should be firmly attached to the body.

Roast Grouper and Vegetables in Parchment Packets

Grouper is flavorful, meaty, and forgiving during longer cooking times. Fresh cod or monkfish are great alternatives.

4 (7-ounce) grouper fillets

1 teaspoon sea salt, divided

1 teaspoon ground black pepper, divided

1 small red onion, peeled and thinly sliced

½ medium green bell pepper, seeded and sliced

1 pint cherry tomatoes, chopped

1 medium zucchini, trimmed and sliced

1 tablespoon minced garlic

2 tablespoons extra-virgin olive oil

¼ cup dry white wine

8 large fresh basil leaves

1 teaspoon dried Greek oregano

SERVES 4

Per Serving:

Calories	295
Fat	9g
Sodium	698mg
Carbohydrates	9g
Fiber	2g
Sugar	4g
Protein	41g

1 Pat fillets dry with a paper towel and season with ½ teaspoon each salt and black pepper. Set aside.

2 In a medium bowl, combine onion, bell pepper, tomatoes, zucchini, garlic, oil, and wine. Toss to combine and season with remaining ½ teaspoon each salt and black pepper.

3 Preheat oven to 400°F.

4 Cut four pieces of parchment paper (about three times the size of each fillet) and place them on a flat surface. Set a fillet in the middle of each sheet and top with ¼ of the vegetable mixture and 2 basil leaves. Sprinkle with oregano.

5 Fold the sides of one sheet of parchment up toward the middle and fold the two pieces to form a seal in the middle. Twist the ends and secure each end with butcher's twine. Repeat with remaining three packets.

6 Place packets on a large baking sheet and bake for 35 minutes.

7 Carefully transfer packets to dinner plates and cut them open at the table.

Mediterranean Seafood Roast

SERVES 8

Per Serving:

Calories	374
Fat	29g
Sodium	755mg
Carbohydrates	4g
Fiber	1g
Sugar	1g
Protein	22g

The marinade becomes the sauce in this easy sheet pan recipe. Lobster tails are widely available at supermarkets, but if you can't find them, add more shrimp, scallops, and mussels. Don't forget to include bread on your shopping list!

⅓ cup lemon juice

¼ cup minced red onion

1 clove garlic, peeled and minced

1 cup extra-virgin olive oil

½ teaspoon sea salt

¼ teaspoon crushed red pepper flakes

1 cup diced fresh fennel

¼ cup ouzo

4 (5-ounce) lobster tails, split in half

12 jumbo shrimp, peeled and deveined

8 large sea scallops

1 pound mussels, scrubbed and beards removed

½ cup chopped fresh parsley

1 medium lemon, cut into wedges

1 Preheat broiler and set rack on the second position from the top. Line a large baking sheet with parchment paper.

2 In a medium bowl, stir together lemon juice, onion, and garlic. While stirring, gradually add oil. Add salt, pepper flakes, fennel, and ouzo and stir to combine.

3 Place lobster, shrimp, and scallops on prepared baking sheet. Drizzle ¾ of the marinade over seafood and toss to combine. Set aside remaining marinade.

4 Broil for 5 minutes. Remove baking sheet from oven, add mussels, and return to oven. Broil until mussel shells open up, about 3 minutes.

5 Remove from oven and drizzle with reserved marinade. Top with parsley and serve with lemon wedges.

Baked Octopus and Eggplant

If you can't find small eggplant, look for Japanese eggplant at your grocer or nearby Asian market. They are available all year and are never bitter. Most fishmongers now carry frozen octopus, an excellent product that only needs to be defrosted overnight in the refrigerator.

SERVES 8	
Per Serving:	
Calories	358
Fat	17g
Sodium	1,179mg
Carbohydrates	14g
Fiber	3g
Sugar	5g
Protein	36g

4 small eggplants, trimmed and thickly sliced

1¼ teaspoons sea salt, divided

1 teaspoon ground black pepper, divided

½ cup olive oil

2 cups marinara sauce

4 whole allspice berries

2 bay leaves

1 (2-pound) cooked octopus, beak removed and tentacles separated

1 cup chopped fresh parsley

1 teaspoon dried Greek oregano

1 Preheat oven to 400°F.

2 Place eggplant slices in a large roasting pan and season with ¾ teaspoon salt and ½ teaspoon pepper. Roast for 15 minutes or until just soft.

3 Remove from oven and add oil, marinara, allspice berries, and bay leaves. Stir to combine. Add octopus and sprinkle with remaining ½ teaspoon each salt and pepper. Return pan to oven and roast for 45–50 minutes or until sauce is thick and octopus turns a deep burgundy color.

4 Remove and discard bay leaves and allspice berries. Garnish with parsley and oregano before serving.

Sheet Pan Gnocchi and Shrimp

SHELF-STABLE GNOCCHI

Keep a few packages of shelf-stable gnocchi on hand for those days when you need a quick and easy dinner idea. These sturdy little nuggets can be a great addition to a sheet pan dinner, but you can also pan-fry them in a skillet. Just heat a couple of tablespoons of olive oil in a large skillet over medium-high heat. Add the gnocchi in a single layer, cover, and cook for 2–4 minutes. Then uncover and cook, stirring, for another 3 minutes or until crisp and golden. No need to boil them at all!

Keep a bag of shelf-stable gnocchi and some frozen shrimp on hand, and you can whip up this simple dinner in minutes. It's so easy to make, and everyone will love it!

1 (16-ounce) package shelf-stable or frozen potato gnocchi

2 tablespoons extra-virgin olive oil

¾ teaspoon salt, divided

¾ teaspoon ground black pepper, divided

1 pound large shrimp, peeled and deveined

1 (24-ounce) jar marinara sauce

½ teaspoon ground star anise

¼ teaspoon crushed red pepper flakes

¼ cup grated graviera or Gruyère cheese

¼ cup crumbled feta cheese

¼ cup chopped fresh parsley

1 Preheat oven to 450°F. Line a large baking sheet with parchment paper.
2 In a large bowl, combine gnocchi, oil, ¼ teaspoon salt, and ¼ teaspoon black pepper. Toss to coat. Transfer to prepared baking sheet and spread gnocchi out in a single layer.
3 Bake for 10 minutes. Remove from oven and stir gnocchi, then bake for 6–7 minutes until lightly browned.
4 Place shrimp in a large bowl and season with remaining ½ teaspoon each salt and black pepper. Add half the marinara sauce, star anise, and pepper flakes and toss to combine. Pour shrimp mixture over gnocchi. Top with remaining sauce and cheeses. Bake for 5–6 minutes until cheese melts.
5 Garnish with parsley before serving.

Spicy Chicken Wings

Be sure to have a cool drink on hand when serving these wings. Try a Greek beer! Serve with some lemon wedges for a fresh hit of citrus.

4 cloves garlic, peeled and minced

1 small yellow onion, peeled and grated

1 tablespoon grated lemon zest

1 tablespoon lemon juice

¼ teaspoon ground cinnamon

¼ teaspoon smoked paprika

½ teaspoon ground allspice

1 teaspoon ground black pepper

½ teaspoon salt

2 tablespoons fresh thyme leaves

¼ cup extra-virgin olive oil

2 pounds chicken wings, patted dry

¼ cup cornstarch

1 In a large bowl, combine garlic, onion, lemon zest, lemon juice, cinnamon, paprika, allspice, pepper, salt, thyme, and oil. Add chicken wings and stir to coat.

2 Marinate wings for at least 4 hours or overnight in the refrigerator.

3 Preheat oven to 425°F. Line a large baking sheet with parchment paper.

4 Remove wings from refrigerator 20 minutes before baking and bring to room temperature. Remove excess marinade from wings and transfer to another large bowl. Add cornstarch and toss to coat evenly.

5 Transfer wings to prepared baking sheet and bake for 25 minutes. Remove from oven, flip wings, and bake for another 25 minutes or until crispy.

6 Serve hot or at room temperature.

SERVES 6

Per Serving:

Calories	293
Fat	21g
Sodium	266mg
Carbohydrates	8g
Fiber	1g
Sugar	1g
Protein	17g

NOT JUST FOR STOCK

Restaurant chefs are known for being resourceful, and they try to avoid tossing out food if it can be used for something else. Chicken wings were traditionally used to make stock. That all changed when the Anchor Bar in Buffalo, New York, was short on food for a catered function and added chicken wings to the menu. Today, chicken wings are so popular that they have now become one of the pricier cuts of chicken. (But they're still worth it.)

Sheet Pan Chicken Gyro

SERVES 6

Per Serving:

Calories	108
Fat	5g
Sodium	838mg
Carbohydrates	1g
Fiber	0g
Sugar	0g
Protein	15g

Did you know that you can make gyro with chicken? This sheet pan version is an easy way to enjoy a Greek favorite. As with the pork version, it's great wrapped in pita with fresh vegetables and creamy tzatziki.

6 (3-ounce) boneless, skinless chicken thighs

2 teaspoons sea salt

½ teaspoon ground black pepper

1 teaspoon granulated garlic

1 teaspoon onion powder

1 teaspoon sweet paprika

1 teaspoon dried Greek oregano

1 Preheat oven to 300°F. Line a large baking sheet with parchment paper.

2 Pat chicken dry with a paper towel. Sprinkle both sides with salt, pepper, garlic, onion powder, paprika, and oregano. Place chicken on prepared baking sheet.

3 Roast for 1 hour or until internal temperature reaches 165°F.

4 Allow to cool for 30 minutes. Use a sharp knife to cut into slices and spread out on the baking sheet.

5 Preheat oven to 550°F.

6 Return baking sheet to oven and bake for 5–6 minutes until edges are just crisp. Serve warm or at room temperature.

Sheet Pan Chicken and Potatoes Riganato

Roast chicken with lemons and potatoes is a classic Greek all-in-one meal. Practically every family has their way of making it. This version is both simple and delicious, and it's bound to become a family favorite.

1 (3½-pound) whole chicken, cut into 4 quarters

1 pound baby Yukon Gold potatoes

⅓ cup extra-virgin olive oil

¼ cup lemon juice

2 teaspoons sea salt

½ teaspoon ground black pepper

2 cloves garlic, peeled and minced

2 teaspoons dried Greek oregano

2 bay leaves

½ medium lemon, cut into 4 wedges

1 Preheat oven to 400°F. Line a large baking sheet with parchment paper.

2 Place chicken and potatoes on prepared baking sheet.

3 In a small bowl, whisk together oil, lemon juice, salt, pepper, garlic, and oregano. Pour over chicken and potatoes and toss to coat. Add bay leaves on top of chicken and potatoes.

4 Roast for 50 minutes or until internal temperature reaches 165°F.

5 Remove and discard bay leaves. Serve with lemon wedges.

SERVES 4

Per Serving:

Calories	710
Fat	44g
Sodium	1,324mg
Carbohydrates	23g
Fiber	2g
Sugar	1g
Protein	54g

RIGANATO

"Riganato" is the name given to any dish that contains oregano. Oregano is the most popular herb in Greek cuisine. Greeks put it on almost everything! Greek oregano is bolder and spicier than the Italian variety. You can find dried Greek oregano in most supermarkets.

Roast Chicken Thighs with Tomatoes and Potatoes

SERVES 4

Per Serving:

Calories	578
Fat	37g
Sodium	1,042mg
Carbohydrates	22g
Fiber	3g
Sugar	2g
Protein	39g

Tomatoes are best in the summer, but cherry tomatoes are a reliable product throughout the year. They are small and sweet, and cook quickly. The tomatoes produce a sweet and tangy sauce that complements both chicken and potatoes.

8 (4-ounce) boneless, skin-on chicken thighs, cut in half lengthwise

¼ cup extra-virgin olive oil

1½ teaspoons sea salt, divided

1 teaspoon ground black pepper, divided

1 pint cherry tomatoes

16 small new potatoes, halved

6 cloves garlic, peeled and sliced

2 bay leaves

1 teaspoon fresh thyme leaves

1½ tablespoons lemon juice

1 Preheat oven to 375°F.

2 Place chicken in a large roasting pan and drizzle with oil. Season with 1 teaspoon salt and ½ teaspoon pepper.

3 Place tomatoes, potatoes, garlic, and bay leaves around chicken. Top with thyme and remaining ½ teaspoon each salt and pepper. Drizzle with lemon juice.

4 Roast for 40 minutes. Remove bay leaves. Serve warm.

Balkan Sauerkraut Rice

This is a riff on a traditional Balkan dish that features pickled cabbage. To make this dish more accessible, sauerkraut is used instead. Serve this rice as part of your next Thanksgiving or Christmas feast. It will become a favorite!

1½ cups long-grain rice, rinsed

2½ cups sauerkraut, drained

4 tablespoons unsalted butter, melted

1 small yellow onion, peeled and diced

1½ teaspoons sweet paprika

½ teaspoon smoked paprika

1½ teaspoons sea salt

½ teaspoon ground black pepper

4 cups chicken broth

6 (3-ounce) pork sausages

SERVES 6	
Per Serving:	
Calories	430
Fat	20g
Sodium	1,879mg
Carbohydrates	47g
Fiber	3g
Sugar	3g
Protein	14g

1 Preheat oven to 425°F.

2 In a large roasting pan, combine rice, sauerkraut, butter, onion, sweet paprika, smoked paprika, salt, and pepper. Stir in broth.

3 Bake for 30 minutes. Add sausages and bake for another 20 minutes.

4 Serve immediately.

Baked Sausages and Peppers

Per Serving:

Calories	364
Fat	30g
Sodium	721mg
Carbohydrates	14g
Fiber	4g
Sugar	7g
Protein	10g

EAT MORE PEPPERS

Did you know that peppers are fruits, not vegetables? Peppers originated in Mexico and South America and were introduced to Spain in the late 1400s. They were quickly adopted by and grown in European countries. From there, peppers spread to Africa and Asia.

This dish is similar to a rustic Greek dish called spetsofai. This streamlined sheet pan version makes a hearty and satisfying weeknight meal.

6 (3-ounce) Italian sausages

½ cup extra-virgin olive oil

4 small hot banana peppers, seeded and sliced lengthwise

3 medium red or yellow bell peppers, seeded and sliced

2 medium yellow onions, peeled and sliced

3 cloves garlic, peeled and minced

2 large ripe tomatoes, grated

1 teaspoon sea salt

½ teaspoon ground black pepper

2 teaspoons dried oregano

1 Preheat oven to 375°F. Line a large baking sheet with parchment paper.

2 Place all ingredients on prepared baking sheet. Toss to coat and spread out evenly. Cover with foil and bake for 40 minutes.

3 Uncover and bake for another 15 minutes or until just golden brown.

4 Serve hot.

Sheet Pan Pork Gyro

Traditional pork gyro is slow roasted on a vertical rotisserie. Here's a version of the delicious Greek street food that you can make without a rotisserie. Serve it with warmed pita bread, tzatziki, onions, and tomatoes.

1 tablespoon sugar

3 teaspoons sea salt, divided

1½ teaspoons ground black pepper

2 tablespoons garlic powder

2 tablespoons sweet paprika

1 tablespoon dried Greek oregano

1 teaspoon fresh thyme leaves

1 (3-pound) boneless pork butt

1½ tablespoons lemon juice

1 Combine sugar, 2 teaspoons salt, pepper, garlic powder, paprika, oregano, and thyme in a small bowl. Rub mixture all over pork. Place pork in a covered container and refrigerate for at least 4 hours or overnight.

2 Preheat oven to 500°F.

3 Transfer pork to a large baking sheet and roast for 20 minutes until browned all over. Remove from oven and sprinkle with lemon juice. Remove pork from pan and wrap in a large sheet of parchment paper. Wrap the paper-wrapped pork in foil and return to baking sheet.

4 Reduce oven temperature to 350°F and return pork to oven. Roast for 2 hours or until internal temperature reaches 160°F.

5 Remove from oven and keep covered. Allow to cool for 20 minutes.

6 Preheat broiler.

7 Unwrap pork and break up the meat with your fingers into bite-sized pieces. Place pieces on the baking sheet and sprinkle with remaining 1 teaspoon salt. Broil until meat just begins to crisp, about 7–8 minutes. Serve immediately.

Roast Pork with Sage, Honey, and Thyme

Greek thyme honey is considered one of the best in the world. It gets its intense aroma and rich herbal flavor from the wild thyme that is found all over Greece.

SERVES 8

Per Serving:

Calories	701
Fat	47g
Sodium	520mg
Carbohydrates	17g
Fiber	3g
Sugar	3g
Protein	50g

1 (6-pound) bone-in pork butt

¼ cup orange juice

½ cup extra-virgin olive oil, divided

¼ cup thyme honey

2 tablespoons red wine vinegar

3 tablespoons mild mustard

3 cloves garlic, peeled and smashed

2 tablespoons chopped fresh sage

6 sprigs fresh thyme

3 bay leaves

1 teaspoon dried oregano

1 tablespoon plus 1 teaspoon coarse sea salt, divided

3 teaspoons ground black pepper, divided

6 medium russet potatoes, peeled and quartered

3 medium yellow onions, peeled and quartered

1 stalk celery, trimmed and roughly chopped

1 large carrot, peeled and roughly chopped

1 medium green bell pepper, seeded and roughly chopped

1 medium red bell pepper, seeded and roughly chopped

1 pint cherry tomatoes

1 small dried chili pepper

1½ cups water

1 Place pork in a large zip-top plastic bag. In a medium bowl, combine orange juice, ¼ cup oil, honey, vinegar, mustard, garlic, sage, thyme, bay leaves, oregano, 1 tablespoon salt, and 2 teaspoons black pepper. Stir well, then pour over pork. Seal bag and marinate in refrigerator for at least 2 hours.

2 Preheat oven to 400°F. Remove pork from the refrigerator.

3 Transfer pork and marinade to a large roasting pan. Cover pan with foil and roast for 90 minutes.

4 Place potatoes, onions, celery, carrot, bell peppers, tomatoes, chili pepper, and remaining 1 teaspoon each salt and black pepper in a large bowl. Add remaining ¼ cup oil and toss to coat. Set aside.

5 Remove foil from roasting pan and arrange vegetable mixture around pork. Pour in water. Roast for 45 minutes.

6 Remove and discard bay leaves and thyme sprigs. Allow to rest for 25 minutes before serving.

Sheet Pan Greek-Style Pork Tenderloin with New Potatoes

SERVES 8

Per Serving:

Calories	334
Fat	17g
Sodium	638mg
Carbohydrates	22g
Fiber	4g
Sugar	3g
Protein	25g

Pork tenderloin is a good choice for a weeknight meal because it cooks quickly. If you like your meat a little pink, pork tenderloin is a great cut that can be served medium.

2 (1-pound) pork tenderloins, trimmed

8 tablespoons extra-virgin olive oil, divided

2 teaspoons sea salt, divided

1½ teaspoons ground black pepper, divided

2 cloves garlic, peeled and minced

1½ pounds small new potatoes, halved

1½ pounds fresh green beans, trimmed

3 tablespoons lemon juice

1½ teaspoons dried Greek oregano

1 Preheat oven to 450°F. Line a large baking sheet with parchment paper.

2 Place pork on prepared baking sheet. Pour 2 tablespoons oil over pork and season with 1 teaspoon salt, ½ teaspoon pepper, and garlic. Rub oil and seasonings into pork.

3 Place potatoes and green beans in a large bowl. Add 2 tablespoons oil and toss to coat. Add vegetables to sheet and spread evenly around pork. Season vegetables with remaining 1 teaspoon each salt and pepper.

4 Bake for 25–30 minutes until internal temperature of pork reaches 145°F. Transfer pork to a platter and tent with foil to keep warm.

5 Spread out vegetables to cover the sheet and bake for another 10 minutes.

6 Whisk together lemon juice, oregano, and remaining 4 tablespoons oil in a small bowl.

7 Cut pork into slices and serve with potatoes and beans. Drizzle with lemon-oregano sauce.

Baked Keftedes

You can use a variety of ground meats to make these meat patties. They're also wonderful fried in a skillet: Dredge them in a little flour and fry them in extra-virgin olive oil for a delicious treat.

2 pounds 85/15 ground beef

2 medium yellow onions, peeled and grated

2 (1-ounce) slices bread, soaked in water, squeezed dry, and crumbled

1 tablespoon minced garlic

2 large eggs, beaten

2 teaspoons dried Greek oregano

2 tablespoons chopped fresh parsley

1 teaspoon chopped fresh mint

1/8 teaspoon ground cumin

1 teaspoon salt

3/4 teaspoon ground black pepper

1 Line a large baking sheet with parchment paper.
2 In a large bowl, combine all ingredients and mix well.
3 Use your hands to form meat mixture into sixteen 2½" patties, then place them on prepared baking sheet. Cover with plastic wrap and refrigerate for at least 4 hours or overnight.
4 Preheat oven to 475°F.
5 Remove keftedes from refrigerator and allow about 15 minutes to bring them to room temperature.
6 Bake on the lowest oven rack for 8 minutes. Flip and bake for another 8 minutes. Serve immediately.

SERVES 8

Per Serving:

Calories	242
Fat	13g
Sodium	419mg
Carbohydrates	7g
Fiber	1g
Sugar	2g
Protein	23g

GREEK OREGANO

In Greek, *oregano* means "joy of the mountain." Greek oregano has wider and fuzzier leaves than the common variety. When dried, it has an unmistakable and distinct pungent aroma. Whenever possible, use Greek oregano in your dishes.

Greek Meatballs with Roast Potatoes

Don't let the long list of ingredients scare you—this is actually an easy weeknight dinner!

2 (1-ounce) slices stale bread

½ cup whole milk

6 large Yukon Gold potatoes, peeled and quartered

1 medium yellow onion, peeled and roughly chopped

3 cloves garlic, peeled and smashed

½ medium red bell pepper, seeded and sliced

½ medium green bell pepper, seeded and sliced

½ medium carrot, peeled, halved lengthwise, and sliced

1 cup tomato purée

1 teaspoon sweet paprika

2 bay leaves

1½ teaspoons sea salt, divided

1 teaspoon ground black pepper, divided

1 teaspoon crushed red pepper flakes

3 teaspoons dried Greek oregano, divided

1 cup chicken stock

¼ cup extra-virgin olive oil

½ pound 85/15 ground beef

½ pound ground pork

1 medium yellow onion, peeled and grated

1 clove garlic, peeled and minced

1 large egg

⅛ teaspoon ground allspice

½ teaspoon dried mint

1 tablespoon parsley

SERVES 8

Per Serving:

Calories	343
Fat	15g
Sodium	291mg
Carbohydrates	36g
Fiber	5g
Sugar	6g
Protein	16g

MIX IT UP

Although these meatballs are made with a combination of beef and pork, the recipe can be customized to your taste. Try using all beef, all pork, ground turkey, ground chicken, or even minced salmon or shrimp.

1 Preheat oven to 425°F. Grease a large baking sheet.

2 Place bread in a small bowl and pour in milk. Let bread soak for 5 minutes, then squeeze out as much milk as possible. Set aside.

3 On a large baking sheet, combine potatoes, chopped onion, smashed garlic, bell peppers, carrot, tomato purée, paprika, bay leaves, 1 teaspoon salt, ½ teaspoon black pepper, pepper flakes, 1 teaspoon oregano, and stock. Drizzle with oil. Bake for 30 minutes.

4 Place soaked bread, beef, pork, grated onion, minced garlic, egg, allspice, mint, remaining 2 teaspoons oregano, and remaining ½ teaspoon each salt and black pepper in a large bowl. Mix with your hands and form into palm-sized meatballs.

5 Remove baking sheet from oven and place meatballs on top of potato mixture. Bake for 15–20 minutes until meatballs are browned. Remove and discard bay leaves. Sprinkle with parsley before serving.

Roast Lamb and Potatoes

SERVES 8

Per Serving:

Calories	625
Fat	29g
Sodium	1,483mg
Carbohydrates	55g
Fiber	8g
Sugar	5g
Protein	36g

This is the Mediterranean version of a Sunday roast. Cutting the lamb into chunks reduces the cooking time and makes it easier to portion out. Try goat instead of lamb; it's leaner and milder in flavor.

¼ cup extra-virgin olive oil

1 large yellow onion, peeled and grated

1 tablespoon grated lemon zest

2 tablespoons Dijon mustard

10 sprigs fresh thyme

2 teaspoons dried Greek oregano

4 teaspoons sea salt, divided

2½ teaspoons ground black pepper, divided

1 (3-pound) lamb shoulder, trimmed and cut into 2" pieces

12 cloves garlic, peeled and cut into slivers

12 medium Yukon Gold potatoes, peeled and quartered lengthwise

1 cup chicken stock

3 tablespoons lemon juice

1 In a medium bowl, add oil, onion, lemon zest, mustard, thyme, oregano, 2 teaspoons salt, and 1 teaspoon pepper. Stir until combined.

2 Place lamb in a large container with a lid. Cut small slits in all lamb pieces and insert slivers of garlic in the slits. Pour marinade over meat, cover, and refrigerate for 6–12 hours.

3 Preheat oven to 400°F.

4 Transfer lamb and marinade to a large roasting pan. Season with 1 teaspoon salt and ½ teaspoon pepper and cover pan with foil. Roast for 1½–2 hours until meat is loosened from the bone.

5 In a large bowl, toss potatoes with stock, lemon juice, and remaining 1 teaspoon each salt and pepper. Add to roasting pan.

6 Roast uncovered for 45–50 minutes until potatoes are tender and lamb is deep brown.

7 Remove and discard thyme sprigs. Let rest for 10 minutes before serving.

Chuck Roast with Potatoes

Cooking the roast under foil ensures the meat is moist and tender. Once the roast is uncovered, the direct oven heat will give it color and flavor.

6 large Yukon Gold potatoes, peeled and quartered

1½ cups diced yellow onion

2 cloves garlic, peeled and sliced

½ cup diced red bell pepper

1 cup tomato purée

4 cups beef stock

1 teaspoon dried Greek oregano

1 teaspoon sweet paprika

3 bay leaves

2 teaspoons sea salt, divided

1¾ teaspoons ground black pepper, divided

½ cup extra-virgin olive oil

1 (3½-pound) boneless chuck roast, cut into chunks

1 teaspoon crushed red pepper flakes

SERVES 8	
Per Serving:	
Calories	683
Fat	41g
Sodium	1,183mg
Carbohydrates	31g
Fiber	5g
Sugar	5g
Protein	46g

1 Preheat oven to 425°F.

2 Place potatoes, onion, garlic, bell pepper, tomato purée, stock, oregano, paprika, bay leaves, 1 teaspoon salt, and ¾ teaspoon black pepper in a large roasting pan. Drizzle with oil and toss to coat.

3 Sprinkle beef with remaining 1 teaspoon each salt and black pepper and add to the roasting pan. Cover with foil and roast for 50 minutes. Uncover and roast for another 25–35 minutes until most of the liquid is absorbed, potatoes are crisp, and meat is browned.

4 Remove and discard bay leaves. Sprinkle with pepper flakes before serving.

CHAPTER 4

Dutch Oven and Stockpot Dishes

Artichokes à la Polita

ARTICHOKE SHORTCUT

It can be intimidating to look at an artichoke and figure out how to trim it. But you don't have to do it yourself. Look for trimmed and frozen artichoke hearts in the supermarket freezer section. No need to defrost them. You can add them frozen, and they'll cook in about 20 minutes.

"À la polita" is how Greeks refer to dishes with origins in Constantinople (now Istanbul). This version is popular in springtime when artichokes first appear in markets.

¼ cup extra-virgin olive oil

2 medium yellow onions, peeled and sliced

4 medium red potatoes, peeled and cut into thirds

3 large carrots, peeled and cut into 2" pieces

1 tablespoon tomato paste

12 medium artichokes, peeled, trimmed, halved, and chokes removed

1 teaspoon salt

¾ teaspoon ground black pepper

1 cup thawed frozen or fresh green peas

½ cup chopped fresh dill

1 large lemon, cut into wedges

1 Heat oil in a stockpot or Dutch oven over medium-high heat. Stir in onions, potatoes, and carrots. Reduce heat to medium and cover. Simmer for 15 minutes.

2 Add tomato paste, artichokes, salt, pepper, and enough water to cover. Bring to a boil over high heat, cover pot, and reduce heat to medium. Cook for 10 minutes until artichokes are tender.

3 Gently stir in peas and dill. Remove pot from heat and allow peas to cook in the hot liquid for 5 minutes. Serve hot with lemon wedges.

Okra in Tomato Sauce

Okra contains mucilage, a syrupy substance that helps to thicken a stew like this or a gumbo. Using frozen baby okra saves time and effort. All you need to do is open the bag and toss them in. You don't even need to defrost them first.

2 tablespoons extra-virgin olive oil

2 medium yellow onions, peeled and sliced

1½ pounds fresh or frozen okra, trimmed

½ cup canned plum tomatoes, hand crushed

½ cup chopped fresh parsley

3 cloves garlic, peeled and sliced

6 whole allspice berries

2 cups vegetable stock

2 large russet potatoes, peeled and cut into large chunks

½ teaspoon salt

¼ teaspoon ground black pepper

SERVES 6

Per Serving:

Calories	190
Fat	5g
Sodium	453mg
Carbohydrates	34g
Fiber	6g
Sugar	6g
Protein	6g

1 Heat oil in a stockpot or Dutch oven over medium-high heat. Add onions and sauté for 3 minutes. Cover, reduce heat to medium, and simmer 10 minutes.

2 Add okra, tomatoes, parsley, garlic, allspice berries, and stock. Increase heat to high and bring to a boil.

3 Cover, reduce heat to medium-low, and simmer 15 minutes. Add potatoes and simmer for 20–25 minutes until fork-tender. Stir in salt and pepper and serve.

Classic Minestrone

SERVES 12

Per Serving:

Calories	292
Fat	4g
Sodium	1,022mg
Carbohydrates	47g
Fiber	12g
Sugar	7g
Protein	16g

A traditional Italian vegetarian soup, minestrone can withstand long cooking periods. It tastes even better on the second day.

2 tablespoons olive oil

1 cup minced yellow onion

3 stalks celery, trimmed and chopped

4 cloves garlic, peeled and minced

1 small zucchini, trimmed and chopped

4 cups vegetable broth

2 (14-ounce) cans diced tomatoes, drained

½ cup diced carrots

1 cup red wine (Chianti or cabernet sauvignon)

2 (6-ounce) cans tomato paste

2 tablespoons minced fresh parsley

1½ teaspoons dried oregano

1 teaspoon salt

½ teaspoon ground black pepper

1 teaspoon garlic powder

½ teaspoon Italian seasoning

2 (15-ounce) cans red kidney beans, drained and rinsed

2 (15-ounce) cans cannellini beans, drained and rinsed

1 (28-ounce) can Italian-style green beans

1 cup orzo, ditalini, or other small pasta

4 cups baby spinach

1 Heat oil in a stockpot or Dutch oven over medium-high heat. Sauté onion, celery, garlic, and zucchini for 3–5 minutes until onion is translucent.

2 Add broth, tomatoes, carrots, wine, tomato paste, parsley, oregano, salt, pepper, garlic powder, and Italian seasoning. Bring to a boil, then cover and reduce heat to low. Simmer for 1½ hours. Add kidney beans, cannellini beans, and green beans. Simmer for 30 minutes.

3 Add orzo and cook for 10–15 minutes until tender. Remove from heat and stir in spinach.

4 Serve hot.

Arakas Laderos (Greek-Style Peas)

SERVES 4

Per Serving:

Calories	228
Fat	14g
Sodium	384mg
Carbohydrates	21g
Fiber	7g
Sugar	7g
Protein	7g

This vegetarian dish of green peas, tomatoes, and mint is one of a group of Greek dishes called ladera, *which means "in oil."*

3 tablespoons extra-virgin olive oil, divided

1 tablespoon unsalted butter

4 scallions, trimmed and thinly sliced

18 ounces fresh or frozen green peas

2 medium tomatoes, grated

3 tablespoons chopped fresh dill

½ teaspoon salt

½ teaspoon ground black pepper

1 cup hot water

1 tablespoon chopped fresh mint

1   Heat 2 tablespoons oil in a large saucepan or Dutch oven over medium heat. Add butter and scallions. Cook for 2 minutes until scallions are softened.
2   Add peas and cook for another 2 minutes.
3   Add tomatoes, dill, salt, pepper, and water. Cover and cook for 30 minutes or until all liquid is absorbed and only the oil remains.
4   Serve warm, topped with mint and remaining 1 tablespoon oil.

Cauliflower Stifado

This is a vegetarian version of stifado, a dish usually made with beef. Stifado in Greek refers to a dish with lots of onions. In this version, pearl onions provide sweetness.

¼ cup extra-virgin olive oil

1 medium head cauliflower, cored and cut into florets

1 medium yellow onion, peeled and sliced

4 cloves garlic, peeled and minced

2 bay leaves

1 large red bell pepper, seeded and chopped

1½ tablespoons tomato paste

3 tablespoons chopped fresh rosemary

1 cup peeled pearl onions

6 small red potatoes, halved

3 cups vegetable stock

¾ teaspoon salt

½ teaspoon ground black pepper

4 cups chopped kale

1 cup pitted Kalamata olives

1 teaspoon dried oregano

1 tablespoon red wine vinegar

SERVES 6

Per Serving:

Calories	343
Fat	19g
Sodium	1,212mg
Carbohydrates	40g
Fiber	6g
Sugar	7g
Protein	5g

THE ORIGINS OF CAULIFLOWER

The cauliflower originally came from Cyprus, a large island in the Eastern Mediterranean, and was known as Cyprus cabbage.

1 Heat oil in a large saucepan or Dutch oven over medium-high heat. Add cauliflower and cook for 5 minutes or until browned. Remove cauliflower with a slotted spoon and set aside.

2 Reduce heat to medium and add yellow onion, garlic, bay leaves, and bell pepper to pot. Cook for 5–6 minutes. Add tomato paste, rosemary, pearl onions, and potatoes. Stir and cook for 1 minute.

3 Add stock, salt, and black pepper. Cover pot and simmer for 20 minutes.

4 Uncover pot and add cauliflower and kale. Cover pot and simmer for 10 minutes until kale wilts. Add olives. Simmer uncovered for 5 minutes until sauce has thickened.

5 Stir in oregano and vinegar. Remove and discard bay leaves. Serve hot.

Chestnut Stifado

SERVES 6

Per Serving:

Calories	353
Fat	15g
Sodium	394mg
Carbohydrates	48g
Fiber	6g
Sugar	12g
Protein	5g

You can now find cooked, vacuum-packed chestnuts online and at many grocery stores. They are tender and sweet and make a great addition to this stew. Serve it with some crusty whole-grain bread.

6 tablespoons extra-virgin olive oil, divided

12 pearl onions, peeled

1 medium yellow onion, peeled and sliced

10 ounces ready-to-eat roasted chestnuts

1 pound cremini or button mushrooms, halved

2 cloves garlic, peeled and smashed

3 large sweet potatoes, peeled and cut into large chunks

3 tablespoons tomato paste

½ cup tomato purée

½ cup dry white wine

3 bay leaves

6 whole allspice berries

¾ teaspoon salt

½ teaspoon ground black pepper

1 tablespoon red wine vinegar

1 Heat 4 tablespoons oil in a stockpot or Dutch oven over medium-high heat. Sauté pearl onions for 5–7 minutes until lightly browned. Add yellow onion, chestnuts, mushrooms, and garlic. Reduce heat to medium. Sauté for 5 minutes.

2 Stir in sweet potatoes, tomato paste, tomato purée, wine, bay leaves, allspice berries, salt, and pepper. Add remaining 2 table-spoons oil and enough hot water to almost cover all the ingredients. Bring to a boil. Reduce heat to low, cover, and simmer for 30–40 minutes until pearl onions and sweet potatoes are fork-tender.

3 Remove from heat and remove and discard bay leaves. Stir in vinegar and serve.

Fassolakia Ladera (Braised Green Beans with Potatoes and Tomatoes)

Fassolakia Ladera can be made with any kind of green beans. The flavorful tomato sauce infuses the long-cooked green beans and potatoes. Add a green salad, and you have dinner!

½ cup extra-virgin olive oil

3 medium yellow onions, peeled and sliced

5 cloves garlic, peeled and sliced

¾ teaspoon salt, divided

3 cups tomato purée

4 whole allspice berries

2 pounds fresh green beans, trimmed

½ cup chopped fresh parsley

¼ cup chopped fresh mint

½ cup chopped fresh dill

6 large russet potatoes, peeled and halved

1 cup hot water

½ teaspoon ground black pepper

SERVES 8

Per Serving:	
Calories	430
Fat	14g
Sodium	433mg
Carbohydrates	71g
Fiber	9g
Sugar	12g
Protein	10g

1 Place oil, onions, garlic, and ¼ teaspoon salt in a large saucepan or Dutch oven. Stir to combine, cover, and cook for 5–7 minutes over medium heat until onions are softened. Add tomato purée and allspice berries and simmer for another 5 minutes.

2 Add green beans, parsley, mint, dill, potatoes, and water. Increase heat to high and bring to a boil. Reduce heat to medium-low and simmer for 45 minutes or until green beans and potatoes are tender. Season with pepper and remaining ½ teaspoon salt.

3 Serve immediately.

Potatoes Yiachni

SERVES 6

Per Serving:

Calories	424
Fat	13g
Sodium	827mg
Carbohydrates	72g
Fiber	6g
Sugar	5g
Protein	9g

CREATE YOUR OWN YIACHNI

The potato, of course, is the star of Potatoes Yiachni, but you can add whatever accents you like to this recipe. Replace some or all of the potatoes with sweet potatoes, switch up the other vegetables according to the season, or add your favorite spices. While it's easy to switch up the ingredients, the beauty of this dish is in its simplicity. Sauté some vegetables, add the remaining ingredients, and let it simmer.

In Greece and Turkey, yiachni *refers to a stew featuring onions, garlic, tomato, herbs, and olive oil and cooked on the stovetop. Vegetarian versions of yiachni are often made during Greek Orthodox fasting periods, when many Christians avoid meat in their diets.*

⅓ cup extra-virgin olive oil

1 medium yellow onion, peeled and roughly chopped

1 small red bell pepper, seeded and sliced

1 small green bell pepper, seeded and sliced

1 medium carrot, peeled, halved lengthwise, and sliced

2 cloves garlic, peeled and smashed

6 large Yukon Gold potatoes, peeled and quartered

¾ cup tomato purée

2 cups vegetable stock

1 teaspoon paprika

2 bay leaves

½ teaspoon crushed red pepper flakes

1 teaspoon dried oregano

1½ teaspoons salt

½ teaspoon ground black pepper

1 Heat oil in a stockpot or Dutch oven over medium-high heat. Sauté onion, bell peppers, and carrot for 5–7 minutes until softened. Add garlic and sauté for 30 seconds. Add potatoes, tomato purée, stock, paprika, bay leaves, pepper flakes, oregano, salt, and black pepper.

2 Bring to a boil, then reduce heat to low and cover. Simmer for 40 minutes, then uncover and cook for 5–10 minutes until sauce is thickened.

3 Remove from heat, remove and discard bay leaves, and cool for 10 minutes before serving.

Ratatouille

There are no limits to the types of vegetables that can be added to ratatouille. Get creative and experiment!

½ teaspoon extra-virgin olive oil

1 small eggplant, trimmed and chopped

1 small zucchini, trimmed and chopped

1 small yellow squash, trimmed and chopped

½ medium leek, trimmed and chopped

1 medium shallot, peeled and minced

2 cloves garlic, peeled and minced

1 medium plum tomato, diced

1 tablespoon chopped fresh thyme

1 cup vegetable stock

¼ cup pitted and chopped Kalamata olives

1 teaspoon ground black pepper

1 Heat oil in a large saucepan or Dutch oven over medium-high heat. Sauté eggplant, zucchini, squash, leek, shallot, and garlic until slightly softened, about 8 minutes.

2 Add tomato, thyme, and stock. Bring to a boil, then reduce heat to low. Cover and simmer for 20 minutes.

3 Add olives and pepper; cook for another 5 minutes. Serve hot or at room temperature.

SERVES 6

Per Serving:

Calories	59
Fat	3g
Sodium	245mg
Carbohydrates	8g
Fiber	2g
Sugar	4g
Protein	2g

EVERYTHING HAS ITS TIME

Traditional eating habits are based on seasonal availability of fresh ingredients and do not rely on canning, preservatives, and refrigeration.

Greek-Style Orzo and Spinach Soup

Lemon zest adds a bright, robust flavor to this simple soup.

2 cloves garlic, peeled and minced

3 tablespoons lemon juice

1 teaspoon grated lemon zest

5 cups low-sodium chicken broth

1 small yellow onion, peeled and thinly sliced

1 cup cubed cooked chicken breast

⅓ cup orzo

4 cups baby spinach

SERVES 6

Per Serving:	
Calories	139
Fat	3g
Sodium	208mg
Carbohydrates	12g
Fiber	1g
Sugar	1g
Protein	17g

1 Place garlic, lemon juice, lemon zest, broth, and onion in a stock-pot or Dutch oven over medium-high heat. Bring to boil, then reduce heat to medium-low. Cover and simmer for 40 minutes.

2 Add chicken, orzo, and spinach and cook for another 10 minutes, stirring occasionally. Serve immediately.

Italian Green Beans with Potatoes

SERVES 6

Per Serving:

Calories	104
Fat	8g
Sodium	256mg
Carbohydrates	8g
Fiber	3g
Sugar	3g
Protein	3g

This is a great way to use up leftover baked or boiled potatoes. Switch up the walnuts in this dish with either almonds or hazelnuts.

1 tablespoon extra-virgin olive oil

1¼ pounds fresh Italian green beans, trimmed

2 cloves garlic, peeled and minced

2 large russet potatoes, peeled, cooked, and diced

½ cup vegetable stock

½ teaspoon dried oregano

¼ cup chopped fresh parsley

½ teaspoon salt

½ teaspoon ground black pepper

¼ cup chopped walnuts, toasted

1 Heat oil in a large saucepan or Dutch oven over medium heat.
2 Add green beans, garlic, potatoes, stock, oregano, parsley, salt, and pepper and stir to combine. Cook for 8–10 minutes or until beans are tender.
3 Sprinkle walnuts over beans and serve.

Pasta Salad with Feta, Sun-Dried Tomatoes, and Spinach

Pasta salads are great for backyard entertaining, picnics, or potluck dinners. Using bow tie pasta makes it easy to grab a forkful of all the ingredients with one stab.

3½ teaspoons salt, divided

1½ cups farfalle (bow tie pasta)

1 cup chopped baby spinach

8 sun-dried tomatoes, sliced

1 cup grated carrot

2 scallions, trimmed and thinly sliced

1 clove garlic, peeled and minced

1 medium dill pickle, diced

⅓ cup extra-virgin olive oil

2 tablespoons red wine vinegar

½ cup plain low-fat Greek yogurt

½ teaspoon ground black pepper

1 teaspoon chopped fresh oregano

¼ cup chopped fresh basil

1 cup diced feta cheese

¼ cup chopped fresh chives

SERVES 8	
Per Serving:	
Calories	169
Fat	10g
Sodium	319mg
Carbohydrates	16g
Fiber	2g
Sugar	3g
Protein	5g

1 Fill a stockpot or Dutch oven two-thirds full with water and place it over medium-high heat. Add 3 teaspoons salt and bring water to a boil. Add pasta and cook for 6–7 minutes or until al dente. Drain pasta in a colander and cool it under cold running water.

2 In a large bowl, combine spinach, tomatoes, carrot, scallions, garlic, and pickle. Add pasta and toss to combine.

3 In a medium bowl, whisk together oil, vinegar, yogurt, pepper, and remaining ½ teaspoon salt. Add dressing to pasta and toss to combine and coat evenly. Toss in oregano, basil, and cheese.

4 Sprinkle salad with chives. Refrigerate until cold or serve at room temperature.

Vegetarian Chili

SERVES 6

Per Serving:

Calories	234
Fat	9g
Sodium	753mg
Carbohydrates	29g
Fiber	10g
Sugar	6g
Protein	10g

LENTILS

Lentils make a good replacement for ground beef. Cooked lentils have a neutral flavor that takes on any seasoning in the dish, and the texture mimics that of ground beef. They are a good, inexpensive source of fiber and protein.

Think of this as "chili con carne-ish." Lentils replace the meat in this warm and comforting bowl.

2 tablespoons extra-virgin olive oil

1 large yellow onion, peeled and chopped

1 small green bell pepper, seeded and chopped

1 small red bell pepper, seeded and chopped

3 cloves garlic, peeled and smashed

1 (28-ounce) can diced tomatoes

1 (15-ounce) can kidney beans, undrained

1 (15-ounce) can brown lentils, drained and rinsed

2 chipotle peppers in adobo sauce, chopped

1 bay leaf

3 tablespoons chili powder

1 teaspoon dried oregano

½ teaspoon salt

½ teaspoon ground black pepper

1 Heat oil in a large saucepan or Dutch oven over medium-high heat. Sauté onion and bell peppers for 6–8 minutes until softened. Add garlic and sauté 1 minute.

2 Stir in tomatoes, beans, lentils, chipotle peppers, bay leaf, chili powder, oregano, salt, and black pepper. Bring to a boil, then reduce heat to medium-low.

3 Simmer for 30–40 minutes until most of the liquid has been absorbed.

4 Remove and discard bay leaf before serving.

Mussels Saganaki

This mussel dish is a specialty of Thessaloniki, Greece, where much of the local cuisine is spicy. Use sweet peppers if you wish to tone down the heat.

2 tablespoons extra-virgin olive oil

1 medium-sized hot banana pepper, seeded and thinly sliced

2 medium tomatoes, chopped

½ teaspoon salt

1 pound fresh mussels, scrubbed and beards removed

⅓ cup crumbled feta cheese

2 teaspoons dried oregano

1 Heat oil in a stockpot or Dutch oven over medium heat. Add pepper, tomatoes, and salt and sauté for 2 minutes.

2 Add mussels and cover. Increase heat to medium-high and steam mussels for 5–6 minutes. Discard any mussels that haven't opened.

3 Add cheese and oregano and shake the pan to combine them into the sauce. Serve hot.

SERVES 2

Per Serving:

Calories	300
Fat	21g
Sodium	988mg
Carbohydrates	12g
Fiber	4g
Sugar	5g
Protein	16g

BEARDED MUSSELS

A clump of hair-like membranes protrudes from the shell of mussels. These sticky membranes are called "beards," and they're what mussels use to attach themselves to surfaces. If the mussels you buy have beards, you simply need to pull them off before cooking. However, most farm-raised mussels are debearded before being sold. All they need is a quick rinse in a colander. The most important thing to do is to discard any mussels that have broken shells or do not open when cooked.

Seafood and Cilantro Soup

SERVES 6

Per Serving:

Calories	106
Fat	3g
Sodium	1,215mg
Carbohydrates	4g
Fiber	0g
Sugar	1g
Protein	13g

This quick-to-make soup is full of lively, fresh summertime flavors.

1 teaspoon olive oil

1 medium red onion, peeled and diced

2 quarts seafood broth or fat-free chicken broth

¼ cup dry white wine

6 large bay scallops

4 ounces lobster meat, roughly chopped

6 small (35/45) shrimp, peeled and deveined

¼ cup chopped fresh cilantro

1 teaspoon lime juice

1 teaspoon ground black pepper

1 Heat oil in a stockpot or Dutch oven over medium-high heat. Sauté onion for 5 minutes or until softened. Add broth and wine and bring to a boil. Reduce heat to medium and cook for 30 minutes.

2 Add scallops and lobster and cook for 10 minutes or until opaque. Stir in shrimp, cilantro, lime juice, and pepper. Simmer for 3 minutes or until shrimp turn pink. Remove from heat and allow to rest for 5 minutes before serving.

Seafood Chowder

Use whatever seafood is fresh and available at your fishmonger for this easy-to-make, thoroughly satisfying soup. If you like the broth even thicker, stir in a mixture of 3 tablespoons cornstarch diluted in 3 tablespoons cold water at the end of cooking.

2 tablespoons olive oil

1½ cups diced yellow onion

1 cup diced celery

1 cup diced carrot

½ cup diced green bell pepper

½ cup diced red bell pepper

3 cups diced potatoes

¼ cup dry white wine

3 bay leaves

11 cups chicken or seafood stock

½ pound small shrimp, peeled and deveined

½ pound bay scallops

1 pound cod, haddock, grouper, or halibut fillets, cut into bite-sized pieces

1 cup heavy cream

2 teaspoons sea salt

1 teaspoon ground black pepper

½ cup chopped fresh parsley

SERVES 10

Per Serving:

Calories	277
Fat	14g
Sodium	1,662mg
Carbohydrates	16g
Fiber	2g
Sugar	4g
Protein	21g

1 Heat oil in a stockpot or Dutch oven over medium-high heat. Sauté onion for 5 minutes or until translucent.

2 Add celery, carrot, bell peppers, potatoes, wine, and bay leaves. Cook, stirring, for 2 minutes.

3 Add stock and bring to a boil. Reduce heat to low, cover, and simmer for 40 minutes.

4 Stir in shrimp, scallops, and fish and cook, stirring occasionally, for 7–10 minutes until seafood is cooked through. Remove and discard bay leaves. Add cream, salt, and black pepper.

5 Remove from heat and allow to rest 5 minutes. Top with parsley and serve.

Spanish-Style Chickpeas with Cod

SERVES 4

Per Serving:

Calories	369
Fat	16g
Sodium	755mg
Carbohydrates	34g
Fiber	6g
Sugar	5g
Protein	24g

This dish is traditionally made with salt cod, which needs to be soaked overnight. Fresh cod is used here, making this a speedy dish to prepare.

¼ cup extra-virgin olive oil

1 cup diced yellow onion

3 cloves garlic, peeled and minced

1 large russet potato, peeled and diced

½ cup diced red bell pepper

2 cups drained and rinsed canned chickpeas

1 tablespoon red wine vinegar

1 pound cod fillets

1 teaspoon sea salt

½ teaspoon ground black pepper

½ teaspoon smoked paprika

½ cup chopped fresh parsley

1 Heat oil in a large saucepan or Dutch oven over medium-high heat. Sauté onion, garlic, and potato for 5 minutes.

2 Add bell pepper, chickpeas, vinegar, and enough hot water to just cover ingredients. Place cod on top and season with salt and black pepper. Reduce heat to medium-low, cover, and simmer for 30 minutes.

3 Remove from heat and add paprika and parsley. Serve immediately.

Cuttlefish with Saffron and Potatoes

SERVES 6

Per Serving:

Calories	454
Fat	13g
Sodium	1,162mg
Carbohydrates	50g
Fiber	4g
Sugar	3g
Protein	31g

This dish takes inspiration from Spain, while the use of saffron shows a little North African influence. Saffron is an expensive spice, but luckily, only three or four threads are needed for this dish. Cuttlefish can often be found in the frozen seafood section; if you can't find it, its cousin squid will work just as well.

⅓ cup olive oil

1 large yellow onion, peeled and diced

2 pounds cuttlefish, cut into strips

½ cup dry white wine

3 saffron threads

4 large russet potatoes, cubed

5 scallions, trimmed and chopped

1½ teaspoons sea salt

½ teaspoon ground black pepper

⅓ cup chopped fresh dill

2 tablespoons lemon juice

1 Heat oil in a large, heavy-bottomed stockpot or Dutch oven over medium heat. Sauté onion for 5 minutes or until softened. Add cuttlefish and sauté for 10–15 minutes until lightly browned and most of the liquid has cooked down.

2 Add wine and saffron. Cook, stirring, until most of the wine has evaporated.

3 Add potatoes, scallions, and enough water to almost cover contents. Increase heat to high and bring to a boil. Cover, reduce heat to low, and simmer for 40 minutes or until cuttlefish and potatoes are fork-tender.

4 Stir in salt, pepper, dill, and lemon juice. Serve immediately.

Fish Soup Avgolemono

Fish soups are a healthy and versatile way to serve fish and vegetables. This soup is finished with a classic Greek emulsion of beaten eggs and lemon juice.

3 tablespoons extra-virgin olive oil, divided

4 medium yellow onions, peeled and quartered

2 stalks celery, trimmed and diced

3 medium carrots, peeled and sliced

3 large russet potatoes, peeled and roughly chopped

1 teaspoon sea salt

½ teaspoon ground black pepper

9 cups plus 1 tablespoon cold water, divided

2 pounds whitefish fillets, cut into 1" pieces

1 tablespoon cornstarch

2 large eggs

3 tablespoons lemon juice

1 medium lemon, cut into wedges

SERVES 6	
Per Serving:	
Calories	483
Fat	18g
Sodium	533mg
Carbohydrates	45g
Fiber	5g
Sugar	6g
Protein	36g

1 Heat 2 tablespoons oil in a stockpot or Dutch oven over medium heat. Sauté onions, celery, and carrots for 10 minutes or until onions are translucent.

2 Add potatoes, salt, pepper, and 9 cups water and increase heat to high. Bring to a boil. Reduce heat to low, cover, and simmer for 30 minutes. Add fish and simmer covered for 15 minutes.

3 Place cornstarch and remaining 1 tablespoon water in a medium bowl and whisk into a slurry. Add eggs and lemon juice and whisk until smooth. While whisking, very slowly add a ladle of hot stock from the soup to the bowl. Continue whisking and add 2 more ladles of stock. Slowly pour mixture into the soup and stir gently.

4 Pour soup into six bowls and drizzle with remaining 1 tablespoon oil. Serve with lemon wedges.

Corn Chowder with Shrimp

SERVES 6

Per Serving:

Calories	312
Fat	11g
Sodium	660mg
Carbohydrates	36g
Fiber	3g
Sugar	14g
Protein	19g

This sweet and savory chowder packs a spicy kick from the seasoning. You may want to double this recipe!

2 tablespoons extra-virgin olive oil

1 cup diced yellow onion

1 stalk celery, trimmed and diced

1 medium red bell pepper, seeded and diced

1 large russet potato, peeled and grated

1 (5-ounce) can evaporated milk

2 cups whole milk

1 cup low-sodium chicken or vegetable stock

1 (8.75-ounce) can cream-style corn

1 cup fresh or frozen corn kernels

2 teaspoons Old Bay or Cajun seasoning

1 pound medium shrimp, peeled and deveined

½ teaspoon paprika

¼ cup sliced scallions

1 Heat oil in a stockpot or Dutch oven over medium-high heat. Sauté onion, celery, and bell pepper for 5–6 minutes.

2 Add potato, evaporated milk, whole milk, stock, cream-style corn, corn kernels, and seasoning. Bring to a boil, then reduce heat to low. Simmer for 30 minutes, stirring often.

3 Stir in shrimp and simmer for 5 minutes.

4 Ladle into six bowls and top with paprika and scallions before serving.

Avgolemono Soup with Chicken and Rice

Fresh lemon juice and eggs give this soup a lovely yellow color. Try substituting rice with orzo or hand-crushed nests of vermicelli pasta.

10 cups chicken stock

⅓ cup finely diced carrot

⅓ cup finely diced celery

⅓ cup Arborio or Carolina rice

1 teaspoon salt

2 large eggs

3 tablespoons fresh lemon juice

2 cups cooked and chopped skinless chicken breast

1 Add stock to a large stockpot over medium-high heat and bring to a boil. Add carrots, celery, and rice. Boil for 10–15 minutes, then remove from heat. Season with salt.

2 In a large bowl, whisk together eggs and lemon juice. Continuing to whisk vigorously, slowly add a ladle of soup liquid into egg mixture. Continue whisking and slowly add another 3–4 ladles of soup (one at a time) into egg mixture.

3 Slowly stir egg mixture back into soup. Stir in chicken.

4 Let soup cool for 5 minutes before serving.

SERVES 8

Per Serving:

Calories	110
Fat	3g
Sodium	1,516mg
Carbohydrates	7g
Fiber	0g
Sugar	2g
Protein	13g

SOUP FOR DINNER

Whether in Greece, Turkey, Italy, Morocco, Spain, Israel, or neighboring countries, a soup or broth can often be the main meal of the day.

Chicken with Kritharaki

AN AROMATIC ADDITION

If you're feeling adventurous, stir a pinch of ground cinnamon into the sauce at the end. Your kitchen will smell like a Greek restaurant.

The Greek name for orzo is kritharaki, *which means "little barley." In Italy, it's called* risoni, *or "big rice."*

4 (6-ounce) bone-in, skinless chicken thighs

4 (4-ounce) bone-in, skinless chicken legs

1 teaspoon sea salt

½ teaspoon ground black pepper

4 tablespoons extra-virgin olive oil, divided

1½ cups diced yellow onion

1 cup diced green bell pepper

1½ cups orzo

1 cup tomato purée

4 cups chicken stock

2 bay leaves

2 tablespoons grated kefalotyri or Romano cheese

1 Season chicken with salt and pepper.
2 Heat 2 tablespoons oil in a Dutch oven or large saucepan over medium-high heat. Brown chicken pieces in batches for 2 minutes per side. Transfer to a plate and set aside.
3 Reduce heat to medium and add remaining 2 tablespoons oil. Sauté onion and bell pepper for 5–7 minutes until softened.
4 Add orzo and stir for 2 minutes to toast the kernels.
5 Return chicken to Dutch oven. Stir in tomato purée, stock, and bay leaves. Bring to a boil. Reduce heat to medium-low, cover, and simmer for 30 minutes, stirring occasionally.
6 Remove and discard bay leaves and top with cheese before serving.

Greek Roast Chicken and Rice

It's not a coincidence that chicken and rice dishes are popular in many different cultures. The main reason is that the rice absorbs flavor from the juices of the chicken. This recipe is an old-time classic and suitable for weekday or weekend meals.

1 (3.5-pound) whole chicken, cut into quarters

1½ teaspoons sea salt, divided

1¼ teaspoons ground black pepper, divided

½ cup diced yellow onion

1 bay leaf

1½ cups parboiled long-grain rice, rinsed

¼ cup extra-virgin olive oil

3 tablespoons lemon juice

3¾ cups chicken stock

1 teaspoon dried Greek oregano

1 Season chicken pieces with 1 teaspoon salt and 1 teaspoon pepper and place in a large Dutch oven. Add onion and bay leaf. Cover chicken with cold water. Bring to a boil over high heat. Reduce heat to medium-low and simmer for 40 minutes, skimming impurities from the surface occasionally.

2 Transfer chicken to a large plate.

3 Preheat oven to 375°F.

4 Pour rice into Dutch oven. Add oil, lemon juice, and stock. Place chicken pieces on top and sprinkle with oregano and remaining ½ teaspoon salt and ¼ teaspoon pepper.

5 Bake uncovered for 45 minutes or until rice has absorbed the liquid and chicken is golden brown. Remove and discard bay leaf. Allow to rest for 5 minutes before serving.

SERVES 4

Per Serving:

Calories	854
Fat	39g
Sodium	1,825mg
Carbohydrates	64g
Fiber	2g
Sugar	2g
Protein	56g

COMMUNITY OVENS

In the old days, kitchens were small, with room only for a stovetop. So on Sundays, homemakers would prepare dinner in a deep roasting vessel and take it to the neighborhood bakery. Traditionally, no bread was baked on Sundays so bakeries could accommodate households bringing their one pan roasts for the oven.

Moroccan-Style Chicken with Green Olives and Lemon

SERVES 6

Per Serving:

Calories	449
Fat	25g
Sodium	1,075mg
Carbohydrates	13g
Fiber	2g
Sugar	7g
Protein	41g

In Morocco, this dish is made in a clay tagine, but you will get great results cooking it in a Dutch oven.

6 (6-ounce) bone-in, skinless chicken thighs

6 (4-ounce) bone-in, skinless chicken legs

1½ teaspoons sea salt, divided

1 teaspoon ground black pepper, divided

¼ cup extra-virgin olive oil

2 cups chopped yellow onion

3 cloves garlic, peeled and minced

6 (½") strips lemon peel

3 tablespoons lemon juice

1 tablespoon ground ginger

½ teaspoon ground cumin

1 teaspoon sweet paprika

½ teaspoon saffron threads

2 bay leaves

1½ cups chicken stock

1 cup green olives

¼ cup raisins

⅛ teaspoon ground cinnamon

½ cup minced fresh parsley

1 Season chicken with 1 teaspoon salt and ½ teaspoon pepper.

2 Heat oil in a Dutch oven over medium-high heat. Brown chicken pieces in batches until golden, 2–3 minutes per side. Drain on a paper towel–lined plate and set aside.

3 Reduce heat to medium and add onion, garlic, lemon peel, lemon juice, ginger, cumin, paprika, saffron, and bay leaves. Sauté for 5–6 minutes until onion is just translucent.

4 Return chicken pieces to pot and add stock. Bring to a simmer, then reduce heat to medium-low. Cover and cook for 45 minutes.

5 Uncover pot and add olives and raisins. Cook uncovered for 10 minutes.

6 Remove and discard bay leaves. Season with cinnamon and remaining ½ teaspoon each salt and pepper. Top with parsley and serve.

Zucchini and Ground Turkey Stew

Ground turkey is a good substitute for ground beef, especially in sauces and stews.

2 tablespoons extra-virgin olive oil

1½ cups diced yellow onion

3 cloves garlic, peeled and minced

1 pound lean ground turkey

½ teaspoon salt

½ teaspoon ground black pepper

¼ cup dry white wine

2 cups tomato purée

3 bay leaves

5 whole allspice berries

6 medium zucchini, trimmed and sliced 1" thick

1 cup water

SERVES 4

Per Serving:

Calories	363
Fat	17g
Sodium	634mg
Carbohydrates	27g
Fiber	6g
Sugar	15g
Protein	29g

1   Heat oil in a large saucepan or Dutch oven over medium-high heat. Sauté onion for 5–7 minutes until translucent. Add garlic and sauté 1 minute.

2   Add turkey, salt, and pepper and cook, stirring constantly, 5 minutes or until meat is browned.

3   Stir in wine and cook for 2 minutes. Add tomato purée, bay leaves, allspice berries, zucchini, and water. Bring to a boil. Reduce heat to medium-low, cover, and simmer for 30 minutes.

4   Remove and discard bay leaves before serving.

Tortellini Soup with Sausage and Spinach

Tortellini are simply small ravioli that are formed into a circular shape. There are many varieties of tortellini fillings, from meat to cheese to vegetables...choose your favorite!

1 pound Italian sausage, casings removed

2 tablespoons extra-virgin olive oil

1 large yellow onion, peeled and diced

3 cloves garlic, peeled and minced

½ cup finely diced carrot

½ cup finely diced celery

2 cups crushed tomatoes

4 cups chicken stock

1 bay leaf

1 teaspoon sea salt

½ teaspoon ground black pepper

1 (9-ounce) package fresh cheese tortellini

1 cup heavy cream

6 cups baby spinach

½ cup grated Parmesan cheese

SERVES 6	
Per Serving:	
Calories	525
Fat	35g
Sodium	1,741mg
Carbohydrates	34g
Fiber	4g
Sugar	8g
Protein	20g

1 Place sausage in a stockpot or Dutch oven over medium-high heat. Brown for 5 minutes, using a wooden spoon to break up sausage into bite-sized pieces.

2 Add oil, onion, garlic, carrot, celery, tomatoes, stock, bay leaf, salt, and pepper. Bring to a boil, then reduce heat to medium-low. Cook uncovered for 15 minutes. Stir in tortellini and cream and simmer for 5 minutes.

3 Remove from heat. Remove and discard bay leaf. Stir in spinach until just wilted. Serve with cheese sprinkled on top.

Caldo Verde

SERVES 8

Per Serving:

Calories	269
Fat	17g
Sodium	1,520mg
Carbohydrates	20g
Fiber	2g
Sugar	3g
Protein	11g

PORTUGUESE CHOURIÇO VERSUS SPANISH CHORIZO

Chouriço and chorizo are both cured sausages, usually made with pork shoulder, paprika, black pepper, garlic, and salt. The proportions of the ingredients differ between the two, however. Chorizo has more paprika, and chouriço has more garlic and black pepper. Also, the type of paprika used is different. Chorizo is made with smoked paprika, and chouriço is made with sweet paprika.

This comforting soup is Portugal's national dish. It literally means "green soup." Try to find Portuguese chouriço, which is a cured pork sausage. If you can't find it, you can substitute Spanish chorizo, but it won't be as authentic. Serve this soup with crusty bread and white wine.

8 cups chicken stock

1 teaspoon salt

2 cloves garlic, peeled and smashed

2 large yellow onions, peeled and quartered

1½ pound russet potatoes, peeled and cut into chunks

3 tablespoons extra-virgin olive oil, divided

1 (8-ounce) link chouriço

2 cups water

2 cups finely shredded kale

1 In a stockpot or Dutch oven over medium-high heat, combine stock, salt, garlic, onions, potatoes, 2 tablespoons oil, chouriço, and water. Bring to a boil, then reduce heat to medium and simmer for 45–50 minutes until potatoes are tender when pierced with a fork.

2 Remove chouriço; slice thinly and set aside.

3 Remove from heat and purée soup in an immersion blender or in batches in a blender until smooth, then return to pot.

4 Stir in kale and cook over medium heat for 5 minutes or until kale is wilted.

5 To serve, ladle the soup into eight bowls and garnish each with a few slices of chouriço. Drizzle with remaining 1 tablespoon oil.

Braised Lamb Shanks

Lamb shanks are affordable and delicious. As long as you cook them slowly, they will reward you with falling-off-the-bone tender meat. Many butchers carry lamb shanks, but you may also find them in the frozen section at your local grocer.

4 (14-ounce) lamb shanks

1½ teaspoons salt, divided

1½ teaspoons ground black pepper, divided

¼ cup olive oil

½ cup dry red wine

3 tablespoons tomato paste

1 large yellow onion, peeled and roughly chopped

6 cloves garlic, peeled and smashed

1 large carrot, peeled and roughly chopped

1 stalk celery, trimmed and roughly chopped

3 bay leaves

8 whole allspice berries

12 sprigs fresh thyme

3 cups hot chicken stock

SERVES 4

Per Serving:

Calories	573
Fat	28g
Sodium	1,695mg
Carbohydrates	11g
Fiber	2g
Sugar	5g
Protein	61g

1 Season lamb shanks with 1 teaspoon salt and 1 teaspoon pepper. Heat oil in a large, oven-safe Dutch oven over medium-high heat. Add shanks and brown on all sides, 2–3 minutes per side.

2 Add wine and deglaze by using a wooden spoon to scrape up any browned bits from the bottom of the pot. Stir in tomato paste, onion, garlic, carrot, celery, bay leaves, allspice berries, thyme, and stock. The shanks should be covered halfway with the stock mixture.

3 Season with remaining ½ teaspoon each salt and pepper. Cover, reduce heat to medium-low, and braise for 1½–2 hours until shanks are fork-tender. Remove shanks from pot and set aside.

4 Transfer the braising liquid to a gravy separator and skim off and discard most of the fat. Remove and discard allspice berries, bay leaves, and thyme sprigs. Pour mixture into a food processor and purée until smooth.

5 Return shanks to pot and cover with purée. Serve warm.

WINE IN COOKING

Don't use cooking wines—they have a high salt content and don't taste very good! Use a full-bodied red wine that you would drink with dinner. You don't have to spend a lot—ordinary table wines are usually more than sufficient for cooking purposes.

Braised Lamb Ragu

When you remove the lamb from the pot, it can be shredded with two forks for a texture similar to pulled pork.

2 pounds boneless lamb shoulder, cut into large pieces

2 teaspoons sea salt, divided

1 teaspoon ground black pepper, divided

¼ cup olive oil

1 large yellow onion, peeled and diced

2 medium carrots, peeled and diced

2 stalks celery, trimmed and diced

4 cloves garlic, peeled and minced

1 tablespoon chopped fresh parsley

3 bay leaves

5 whole allspice berries

6 sprigs fresh thyme

1 teaspoon dried rosemary

1 tablespoon tomato paste

3 sun-dried tomatoes, minced

1½ cups red wine

2 cups tomato sauce

1 cup beef, veal, or lamb stock

1 pound cooked pappardelle

½ cup heavy cream

1 cup grated Parmesan cheese

1 Season lamb with 1 teaspoon salt and ½ teaspoon pepper. Heat oil in a Dutch oven over medium-high heat. Add lamb in batches and brown for 2 minutes per side. Remove from pot and set aside.

2 Reduce heat to medium-low. Add onion, carrots, celery, garlic, and parsley and sauté for 6–7 minutes until softened.

3 Place bay leaves, allspice berries, thyme, and rosemary on a square piece of cheesecloth. Bring up all four corners and tie with kitchen twine to make a bouquet garni. Place bouquet garni in the pot.

4 Stir in tomato paste and sun-dried tomatoes. Cook, stirring, for 2 minutes. Add wine and simmer for 5 minutes. Increase heat to medium-high and add tomato sauce, stock, and lamb. Bring to a boil. Reduce heat to medium-low and simmer for 1 hour.

5 Add remaining 1 teaspoon salt and ½ teaspoon pepper. Simmer uncovered for 30 minutes. Remove and discard bouquet garni.

6 Remove lamb pieces from sauce and simmer sauce for 20–30 minutes until thickened. Add lamb and pasta. Cook, stirring, for 2 minutes. Stir in cream and cheese. Serve hot.

Lamb Shanks and Beans

Beans are versatile—they can be the star of a hearty vegetarian meal or a worthy supporting player in a meat dish like this one.

¼ cup diced pancetta

1 tablespoon water

½ cup all-purpose flour

4 (14-ounce) lamb shanks

1½ teaspoons sea salt

½ teaspoon ground black pepper

4 tablespoons olive oil, divided

3 medium yellow onions, peeled and diced

1 stalk celery, trimmed and diced

1 medium carrot, peeled and diced

5 cloves garlic, peeled and smashed

½ cup tomato purée

½ cup dry white wine

2 cups chicken stock

2 bay leaves

1 teaspoon smoked paprika

1 teaspoon fresh thyme leaves

1 teaspoon fresh rosemary

2 (15-ounce) cans white beans, drained and rinsed

SERVES 4

Per Serving:

Calories	842
Fat	33g
Sodium	1,964mg
Carbohydrates	55g
Fiber	12g
Sugar	7g
Protein	75g

WHITE BEANS

White beans, which are also called navy beans, Boston beans, or Yankee beans, are small, lightly colored beans that are very mild in taste and work well in a variety of recipes. If you don't have white beans, cannellini beans or northern beans, which are slightly larger, are excellent substitutes.

1. Place pancetta and water in a stockpot or Dutch oven over medium heat. Sauté pancetta until crisp, about 5 minutes. Remove with a slotted spoon and set aside. Reserve any drippings in the pot.

2. Place flour in a shallow bowl. Season shanks with salt and pepper and dredge in flour.

3. Add 2 tablespoons oil to the drippings in the stockpot over medium-high heat. Add shanks and brown on all sides, 2–3 minutes per side. Transfer to a plate and set aside.

4. Add remaining 2 tablespoons oil to the pot. Sauté onions, celery, and carrot for 5–6 minutes until softened. Add garlic and sauté for 1 minute. Return shanks to the pot and add tomato purée, wine, stock, bay leaves, paprika, thyme, and rosemary. If the liquid doesn't cover the shanks, add more stock. Bring to a boil, then reduce heat to low, cover, and simmer for 90 minutes.

5. Uncover the pot and turn over shanks. Add beans, cover, and cook for 30 minutes. Add more stock if the mixture seems dry.

6. Remove from heat. Remove and discard bay leaves. Set aside to rest for 10 minutes before serving.

Beef Kokkinisto with Makaronia

SERVES 8

Per Serving:

Calories	443
Fat	23g
Sodium	828mg
Carbohydrates	28g
Fiber	3g
Sugar	5g
Protein	28g

In Greek, kokkinisto *means "reddened," like the tomato-based sauce in this hearty meal.*

2 pounds chuck beef, cut into large pieces

2 teaspoons sea salt, divided

1 teaspoon ground black pepper, divided

¼ cup olive oil

2 medium red onions, peeled and diced

1 medium carrot, peeled and shredded

4 cloves garlic, peeled and smashed

2 cups puréed plum tomatoes

1 tablespoon tomato paste

½ cup dry red wine

3 bay leaves

6 whole allspice berries

⅛ teaspoon ground cinnamon

1 pound ziti or other short pasta, cooked

1 Season beef with 1 teaspoon salt and ½ teaspoon pepper.
2 Heat oil in a Dutch oven over medium-high heat. Brown meat in batches for 2 minutes per side. Remove from pot and set aside.
3 Reduce heat to medium and add onions, carrot, and garlic. Sauté for 5–6 minutes until softened. Stir in puréed tomatoes, tomato paste, wine, bay leaves, allspice berries, and cinnamon. Return beef to pot. Add enough hot water to almost cover beef. Season with remaining 1 teaspoon salt and ½ teaspoon pepper and bring to a boil.
4 Reduce heat to low and partially cover pot. Simmer for 80–90 minutes, stirring occasionally, until meat is fork-tender.
5 Remove from heat. Remove and discard bay leaves. Stir in pasta and serve immediately.

Fasolakia with Veal

This all-in-one meal is great for the summer months when beans, tomatoes, and fresh herbs are in season.

2 tablespoons extra-virgin olive oil

3 medium yellow onions, peeled and sliced

5 cloves garlic, peeled and sliced

½ cup chopped fresh parsley

¼ cup finely chopped fresh mint

½ cup chopped fresh dill

2 pounds fasolakia (runner beans), trimmed

3 large ripe tomatoes, peeled and grated

1 teaspoon salt

½ teaspoon ground black pepper

2 pounds cooked veal or beef, cut into bite-sized pieces

2 large russet potatoes, peeled and quartered

2 cups hot veal or beef broth

SERVES 8	
Per Serving:	
Calories	444
Fat	16g
Sodium	632mg
Carbohydrates	32g
Fiber	6g
Sugar	8g
Protein	44g

1 Heat oil in a large saucepan or Dutch oven over medium-high heat. Add onions and sauté for 5 minutes or until softened. Add garlic, parsley, mint, dill, fasolakia, and tomatoes. Bring mixture to a boil and then reduce heat to medium-low and cook for 30 minutes. Season with salt and pepper.

2 Add meat, potatoes, and enough broth just to cover ingredients. Cook for 30 minutes or until potatoes are soft and sauce thickens a little. Serve hot.

CHAPTER 5
Slow Cooker Dishes

Baked Eggs with Spinach and Cheese

Per Serving:

Calories	675
Fat	45g
Sodium	929mg
Carbohydrates	41g
Fiber	8g
Sugar	6g
Protein	31g

HERBS AND SPICES

People often confuse herbs with spices. Herbs are green and come from plant leaves. Lavender is the only herb (in Western cooking) that is a flower. Frequently used herbs include parsley, basil, oregano, thyme, rosemary, cilantro, and mint. Spices are roots, tubers, barks, berries, or seeds. These include black pepper, cinnamon, nutmeg, allspice, cumin, turmeric, ginger, cardamom, and coriander.

This dish is excellent for brunch, lunch, or supper. Everyone loves it. Even better, it's easy to put together after a tough day.

1½ cups corn bread crumbs

3 (10-ounce) packages frozen spinach, thawed and drained well

2 tablespoons unsalted butter, melted

½ cup shredded Swiss cheese

½ teaspoon ground nutmeg

½ teaspoon salt

½ teaspoon ground black pepper

1 cup heavy cream

8 large eggs

1 Spray a 4–6-quart slow cooker with nonstick cooking spray. Sprinkle bread crumbs on the bottom.

2 In a medium bowl, mix spinach, butter, cheese, nutmeg, salt, and pepper. Stir in cream. Spread spinach and cheese mixture on top of bread crumbs.

3 Using the back of a tablespoon, make eight depressions in spinach mixture. Break open eggs and place 1 egg in each hole.

4 Cover and cook on low for 3 hours or on high for 1½–2 hours until yolks are cooked through but not hard.

Vegetable and Chickpea Stew with Lemon Couscous

This easy-to-make stew works equally well for a light supper or a healthful vegetarian lunch.

1 (15-ounce) can chickpeas, drained and rinsed

2 large carrots, peeled and cut into 1" pieces

1 large yellow onion, peeled and chopped

1 (14.5-ounce) can diced tomatoes

¼ cup low-sodium vegetable broth

1 teaspoon ground cumin

1 teaspoon ground turmeric

1 teaspoon hot smoked paprika

2 cups boiling water

2 teaspoons lemon juice

1 cup couscous

¼ cup chopped fresh parsley

1 Place chickpeas, carrots, onion, and tomatoes in a 4–6-quart slow cooker. Add broth, cumin, turmeric, and paprika. Stir well. Cover and cook on high for 3½ hours.

2 Combine water, lemon juice, and couscous in a medium bowl with a lid. Cover tightly and set aside for 5 minutes, then fluff with a fork.

3 Uncover slow cooker and stir in couscous.

4 Garnish with parsley before serving.

SERVES 4

Per Serving:

Calories	309
Fat	2g
Sodium	284mg
Carbohydrates	59g
Fiber	9g
Sugar	8g
Protein	12g

MAKE CHICKPEAS A STAPLE IN YOUR KITCHEN

Keep cans of chickpeas and other beans in your pantry to use whenever you need an easy and inexpensive meatless option for lunch or for dinner. Chickpeas are great in soups, stews and salads. Roasted, salted, and seasoned, they also make a satisfying snack.

Tomato and Goat Cheese Breakfast Casserole

Per Serving:

Calories	174
Fat	11g
Sodium	356mg
Carbohydrates	5g
Fiber	1g
Sugar	3g
Protein	13g

TOMATOES

It's hard to imagine Mediterranean cuisine without tomatoes. Their bright flavor and rich color make them a staple ingredient in most dishes. The tomato came to Europe via explorer Hernán Cortés in the 1500s after he discovered the Aztecs eating them.

Tomatoes and oregano pair elegantly with goat cheese to create a luscious casserole that works just as well for a light dinner as it does for a weekend brunch.

8 large eggs

1 cup low-fat milk

½ teaspoon salt

1 teaspoon ground black pepper

2 cups halved cherry tomatoes

¼ cup chopped fresh oregano

½ cup crumbled goat cheese

1 teaspoon extra-virgin olive oil

1 In a large bowl, whisk together eggs, milk, salt, and pepper until combined. Stir in tomatoes, oregano, and cheese; mix well again.

2 Grease a 4–5-quart slow cooker with oil.

3 Pour egg mixture into slow cooker, cover, and cook on low for 4–6 hours or on high for 2–3 hours. The casserole is done when a knife inserted into the center comes out clean. Serve hot.

Cannellini Beans with Bacon, Rosemary, and Thyme

These beans are so creamy and decadent, they'll be requested over and over again.

SERVES 16

Per Serving:

Calories	205
Fat	1g
Sodium	130mg
Carbohydrates	34g
Fiber	14g
Sugar	1g
Protein	15g

2 pounds dried cannellini beans, soaked overnight, drained, and rinsed

2 cups low-sodium chicken broth

½ teaspoon salt

½ teaspoon ground white pepper

1 tablespoon chopped fresh rosemary

1 tablespoon chopped fresh thyme

4 slices cooked bacon, chopped

1 Place beans, broth, salt, pepper, rosemary, and thyme in a 4–6-quart slow cooker. Cover and cook on low for 6–8 hours.

2 Top beans with bacon before serving.

Garlic and Artichoke Pasta

Artichoke hearts give this sauce a unique and savory flavor that is perfect for pasta or rice.

2 (14.5-ounce) cans diced tomatoes with basil, oregano, and garlic

2 (14-ounce) cans artichoke hearts, drained and quartered

6 cloves garlic, peeled and minced

½ cup heavy cream

3 cups pasta, cooked

1 Pour tomatoes, artichokes, and garlic into a 4–6-quart slow cooker. Cover and cook on high for 3–4 hours or on low for 6–8 hours.

2 About 20 minutes before serving, stir in cream. Serve over pasta.

SERVES 6

Per Serving:

Calories	246
Fat	8g
Sodium	447mg
Carbohydrates	34g
Fiber	3g
Sugar	3g
Protein	8g

CAN'T FIND SEASONED CANNED TOMATOES?

If you can't find diced tomatoes with herbs and spices in your grocery store, use regular diced tomatoes and add 2 teaspoons of Italian seasoning to your sauce.

Risotto and Greens

SERVES 4

Per Serving:

Calories	382
Fat	6g
Sodium	665mg
Carbohydrates	56g
Fiber	6g
Sugar	4g
Protein	17g

EAT MORE GREENS

Leafy green vegetables aren't just for salads. They make a delicious and healthy addition to almost any main dish. Slightly bitter greens, like baby arugula, are especially good for offsetting the richness of creamy, cheesy risotto.

This risotto makes a beautiful side dish for meat, chicken, or pork.

1 teaspoon olive oil

1 cup Arborio rice

1 large red onion, peeled and finely diced

2 large leeks (white and pale green parts only), trimmed and chopped

2 (14.5-ounce) cans low-sodium chicken broth

1 cup dry white wine

1 (14.5-ounce) can cannellini beans, drained and rinsed

½ teaspoon salt

½ teaspoon ground white pepper

½ cup shredded Parmesan cheese

1 cup baby arugula

1 Grease a 4–6-quart slow cooker with oil. Add rice, onion, leeks, broth, wine, beans, salt, and pepper. Cover and cook on high for 2 hours. If risotto isn't creamy and cooked through, cook for another 30 minutes.

2 Add cheese and arugula and stir well. Serve immediately.

Lemon Garlic Green Beans

Lemon zest and sliced garlic add a fresh and bright flavor to these slow cooked green beans.

1½ pounds fresh green beans, trimmed

3 tablespoons olive oil

3 large shallots, peeled and cut into thin wedges

6 cloves garlic, peeled and sliced

1 tablespoon grated lemon zest

½ teaspoon salt

½ teaspoon ground black pepper

½ cup water

SERVES 4	
Per Serving:	
Calories	171
Fat	11g
Sodium	306mg
Carbohydrates	19g
Fiber	6g
Sugar	8g
Protein	4g

1 Spray a 4–6-quart slow cooker with nonstick cooking spray. Place beans in slow cooker. Add remaining ingredients over beans.

2 Cover and cook on high for 4–6 hours or on low for 8–10 hours.

Slow Cooker Greek-Style Lima Beans

SERVES 4

Per Serving:

Calories	309
Fat	14g
Sodium	893mg
Carbohydrates	37g
Fiber	9g
Sugar	2g
Protein	11g

Most grocery stores now have a vast variety of canned legumes, but you can use another type of white beans if you can't find canned limas.

¼ cup olive oil

2 (15-ounce) cans lima beans, drained and rinsed

1 cup minced yellow onion

½ medium carrot, peeled and grated

3 cloves garlic, peeled and minced

3 bay leaves

1 teaspoon smoked paprika

½ teaspoon ground allspice

2 tablespoons tomato paste

1 cup boiling water

1 tablespoon ketchup

1 teaspoon sea salt

½ teaspoon ground black pepper

¼ cup chopped fresh parsley

2 tablespoons chopped fresh dill

1 Place oil, beans, onion, carrot, garlic, bay leaves, paprika, allspice, tomato paste, and water in a 4–6-quart slow cooker. Stir to combine. Cover and cook on low for 3 hours.

2 Uncover and stir in ketchup, salt, and pepper. Remove and discard bay leaves.

3 Top with parsley and dill and serve immediately.

Slow Cooker Pasta Fagioli

The name of this all-time classic Italian cuisine is literally trans-lated to "pasta and beans." Cannellini beans are traditionally used, but you can swap another small white bean if you prefer. This slow cooker preparation is as good as any stovetop version and it reheats well should you have leftovers.

4 (3-ounce) mild Italian sausages, casings removed

1 cup minced yellow onion

1 cup minced carrot

½ cup minced celery

3 cloves garlic, peeled and minced

2 cups tomato purée

1 cup diced tomato

2 (15-ounce) cans cannellini beans, drained and rinsed

4 cups chicken stock

2 bay leaves

½ teaspoon dried rosemary

2 teaspoons dried oregano

¾ cup ditalini

1½ teaspoons sea salt

½ teaspoon ground black pepper

2 tablespoons extra-virgin olive oil

⅓ cup grated Parmesan cheese

1 Place sausages in a 4–6-quart slow cooker and break them up with a wooden spoon.

2 Add onion, carrot, celery, garlic, tomato purée, diced tomato, beans, stock, bay leaves, rosemary, and oregano. Cover and cook on high for 5–6 hours.

3 Uncover and stir in pasta, salt, and pepper. Cover and cook on high for another 30 minutes. Remove and discard bay leaves.

4 Ladle into six bowls, drizzle with oil, and sprinkle with cheese before serving.

SERVES 6

Per Serving:

Calories	344
Fat	15g
Sodium	1,766mg
Carbohydrates	35g
Fiber	7g
Sugar	6g
Protein	18g

PASTA AND SLOW COOKING

Pasta is a great addi-tion to slow cooked meals, but it shouldn't be added at the begin-ning of cooking. Add uncooked pasta to the slow cooker 30–60 min-utes before serving.

Slow Cooker Minestrone Soup

SERVES 8

Per Serving:

Calories	236
Fat	9g
Sodium	1,370mg
Carbohydrates	30g
Fiber	4g
Sugar	7g
Protein	10g

This recipe is perfect for the busy cook. You can go about your busy day without having to constantly check if the soup is ready.

¼ cup extra-virgin olive oil

2 cups diced yellow onion

3 medium carrots, peeled and sliced

2 stalks celery, trimmed and sliced

4 cloves garlic, peeled and minced

4 cups thinly sliced napa or savoy cabbage

2 (15-ounce) cans navy beans, drained and rinsed

1 (14.5-ounce) can diced tomatoes

5 cups vegetable stock

4 sprigs fresh thyme

2 bay leaves

1 teaspoon dried oregano

2 teaspoons sea salt

1 teaspoon ground black pepper

2 cups trimmed fresh green beans

½ cup grated Parmesan cheese

1 Place oil, onion, carrots, celery, garlic, cabbage, beans, tomatoes, stock, thyme, bay leaves, oregano, salt, and pepper in a 4–6-quart slow cooker. Cover and cook on high for 3½ hours.

2 Add green beans; cover and cook on high for another 30 minutes.

3 Uncover and remove and discard bay leaves and thyme sprigs. Top with cheese before serving.

Slow Cooker Paella

Using a slow cooker to make paella really helps to develop the deep and delicious flavors of this popular Spanish dish.

1 (14.5-ounce) can diced tomatoes

1 medium red onion, peeled and finely diced

2¼ cups low-sodium chicken broth

½ teaspoon crushed saffron threads or ½ teaspoon ground turmeric

½ teaspoon smoked paprika

½ pound andouille sausage, halved and sliced

6 (3-ounce) boneless, skinless chicken thighs

1½ cups long-grain white rice

1 cup thawed frozen baby peas

6 large cooked shrimp, peeled and deveined

1 Place tomatoes, onion, broth, saffron, and paprika in a 4–6-quart slow cooker. Add sausage and chicken. Cover and cook on high for 4 hours.

2 Uncover and stir in rice and peas. Cover and cook on high for 1 hour or until rice is tender and liquid is absorbed. Add shrimp, cover, and cook for another 30 minutes.

3 Serve immediately.

SERVES 6

Per Serving:

Calories	426
Fat	10g
Sodium	614mg
Carbohydrates	50g
Fiber	3g
Sugar	5g
Protein	32g

SAFFRON

Saffron is a spice derived from the dried stigmas of crocus plants. The crocus must be picked by hand so that the delicate stigmas are kept intact. Because of this, saffron is the most expensive spice in the world. Thankfully, a little goes a long way to add rich flavor and bright color to a dish.

Calamari with Spinach and Green Olives

There are two ways to cook calamari: hot and fast or low and slow. With the slow method, you can be sure the squid will be fork-tender.

2 pounds squid, cleaned and tubes cut into thick rounds

1 cup diced yellow onion

1 cup diced carrot

1/2 cup diced celery

2 cloves garlic, peeled and minced

1 1/2 cups diced tomatoes

1/4 cup dry white wine

4 cups baby spinach

1/3 cup extra-virgin olive oil

1 cup pitted green olives

1 teaspoon sea salt

1/2 teaspoon ground black pepper

1/2 cup chopped fresh parsley

1 Place squid, onion, carrot, celery, garlic, tomatoes, and wine in a 4–6-quart slow cooker. Stir to combine. Cover and cook on low for 3 hours.

2 Uncover and add spinach, oil, and olives. Cover and cook on low for 1 hour.

3 Season with salt and pepper and top with parsley before serving.

SERVES 6

Per Serving:

Calories	323
Fat	18g
Sodium	849mg
Carbohydrates	14g
Fiber	3g
Sugar	4g
Protein	26g

WHERE TO FIND SQUID

In some coastal areas, you can find fresh squid at the grocery seafood counter. But you're more likely to find it in the freezer section. Frozen squid has been cleaned, and often already cut into rings. If the package includes tentacles, add them to the pot as well.

Slow Cooker Cod in Marinara Sauce

SERVES 4

Per Serving:

Calories	669
Fat	41g
Sodium	2,001mg
Carbohydrates	28g
Fiber	8g
Sugar	11g
Protein	48g

Cod is a hearty whitefish that holds up well to long cooking times. Other types of fish that work well here are grouper and monkfish, but you can use any kind of whitefish. Remember the old saying: "The best fish is the freshest fish."

½ cup extra-virgin olive oil

1 cup sliced yellow onion

4 (8-ounce) cod fillets

1 teaspoon sea salt

½ teaspoon ground black pepper

2 cups tomato sauce

½ cup diced green bell pepper

2 cups sliced white mushrooms

½ cup Kalamata olives

½ cup green olives

3 cloves garlic, peeled and minced

¼ cup dry white wine

1 teaspoon dried oregano

2 bay leaves

½ cup chopped fresh parsley

1 Pour oil into a 4–6-quart slow cooker. Arrange onion slices over oil. Season cod with salt and black pepper and place on top of onion slices.

2 In a medium bowl, combine tomato sauce, bell pepper, mushrooms, olives, garlic, wine, oregano, bay leaves, and parsley. Stir to mix, then pour over cod.

3 Cover and cook on high for 5 hours. Remove and discard bay leaves.

4 Serve immediately.

Slow Cooked Octopus and Pasta

Octopus can be intimidating to many, but with this slow cooker method, it's easy to prepare. The fork-tender meat will win over your family and friends.

1½ tablespoons tomato paste

½ cup hot water

1 (2-pound) octopus, beak removed and tentacles separated

⅓ cup extra-virgin olive oil

1 large yellow onion, peeled and grated

2 cloves garlic, peeled and minced

1 medium carrot, peeled and diced

1 stalk celery, trimmed and diced

½ cup tomato purée

½ cup dry red wine

2 bay leaves

1 (2") cinnamon stick

1½ cups elbow macaroni

1 cup chopped fresh dill

¼ teaspoon salt

¼ teaspoon ground black pepper

SERVES 4	
Per Serving:	
Calories	572
Fat	22g
Sodium	889mg
Carbohydrates	47g
Fiber	4g
Sugar	5g
Protein	41g

1 In a small bowl, stir together tomato paste and water until combined. Transfer to a 4–6-quart slow cooker. Add octopus, oil, onion, garlic, carrot, celery, tomato purée, wine, bay leaves, and cinnamon stick. Stir to combine.

2 Cover and cook on high for 5–5½ hours until tentacles are tender when a knife is inserted.

3 Uncover and add macaroni and enough hot water to cover by 1". Cover and cook for another 30 minutes.

4 Remove and discard bay leaves and cinnamon stick. Stir in dill, salt, and pepper. Serve immediately.

Chicken with Hilopites

Hilopites are a Greek pasta made from flour, eggs, and milk. The dough is rolled out into a large sheet and cut into long, thin strips. The strips are then cut across into small squares.

SERVES 4

Per Serving:

Calories	594
Fat	32g
Sodium	1,050mg
Carbohydrates	26g
Fiber	4g
Sugar	7g
Protein	50g

4 (10-ounce) chicken leg quarters, skin removed

¼ cup olive oil

2 cups sliced yellow onion

1 medium sweet banana pepper, seeded and minced

1 cup tomato passata or 2 cups grated tomatoes

4 cups hot water

2 cups hilopites (square-cut egg noodles)

1 teaspoon sea salt

½ teaspoon ground black pepper

½ cup chopped fresh parsley

1 cup grated Parmesan cheese

1 Place chicken, oil, onion, pepper, passata, and water in a 4–6-quart slow cooker and stir to combine. Cover and cook on high for 3 hours.

2 Uncover and stir in hilopites, salt, and pepper. Cover and cook on high for 45 minutes.

3 Transfer to four plates and top with parsley and cheese before serving.

Slow Cooker Chicken with Summer Vegetables

This dish is best in the summer when your garden is teeming with vegetables. If you wish to make this in the off-season, try Japanese eggplant and sweet potatoes for a nice switch up.

2½ pounds bone-in, skinless chicken thighs and legs

1 large yellow onion, peeled and sliced

3 large russet potatoes, peeled and cut into large chunks

3 medium eggplants, trimmed and cut into ½" rounds

2 large zucchini, trimmed and cut into ½" rounds

3 large tomatoes, grated

5 cloves garlic, peeled and smashed

½ cup extra-virgin olive oil

2 teaspoons sea salt

½ teaspoon ground black pepper

1 teaspoon sweet paprika

3 bay leaves

½ cup chopped fresh parsley

1 teaspoon dried oregano

1 Place chicken, onion, potatoes, eggplants, zucchini, tomatoes, garlic, oil, salt, pepper, paprika, and bay leaves in a 4–6-quart slow cooker. Cover and cook on low for 5 hours.

2 Uncover and remove and discard bay leaves. Stir in parsley and oregano and serve.

SERVES 8

Per Serving:

Calories	456
Fat	20g
Sodium	663mg
Carbohydrates	46g
Fiber	10g
Sugar	13g
Protein	26g

SUMMER AND WINTER SQUASH

You will often hear zucchini and yellow squash referred to as "summer squash." Squash is normally divided into two groups: summer squash and winter squash. Summer squashes have thin skins and soft seeds. Winter squashes have tough skins and hard seeds.

Slow Cooker Apricot Chicken

SERVES 4

Per Serving:

Calories	624
Fat	26g
Sodium	747mg
Carbohydrates	47g
Fiber	2g
Sugar	36g
Protein	49g

This dish balances sweet with savory by using both dried apricots and apricot jam. If you find it a bit too sweet, a splash of wine vinegar at the end will balance out the dish.

8 (6-ounce) bone-in, skinless chicken thighs

1 medium yellow onion, peeled and grated

2 tablespoons olive oil

¼ cup red wine vinegar

2 tablespoons tomato paste

2 tablespoons honey

½ cup apricot jam

12 dried apricots

1 teaspoon sweet paprika

1 teaspoon sea salt

½ teaspoon ground black pepper

2 scallions, trimmed and thinly sliced

1 Place chicken and onion in a 4–6-quart slow cooker. Add oil, vinegar, tomato paste, honey, jam, apricots, and paprika. Cover and cook on low for 6–7 hours.

2 Season with salt and pepper and sprinkle with scallions before serving.

Slow Cooker Pork with Leeks

SERVES 6

Per Serving:

Calories	305
Fat	22g
Sodium	877mg
Carbohydrates	9g
Fiber	2g
Sugar	4g
Protein	19g

Leeks may have some sand or grit in them, so take a close look after slicing them. You may have to rinse them a couple of times.

1½ pounds pork shoulder, trimmed of excess fat and cut into 1" cubes

1 cup minced yellow onion

1 cup thinly sliced leeks

1 cup diced carrot

½ cup tomato purée

¼ cup extra-virgin olive oil

½ teaspoon minced fresh rosemary

2 bay leaves

4 sprigs fresh thyme

½ cup hot water

2 teaspoons sea salt

½ teaspoon ground black pepper

1 Place pork, onion, leeks, carrot, tomato purée, oil, rosemary, bay leaves, thyme, and water in a 4–6-quart slow cooker. Cover and cook on low for 6 hours.

2 Uncover and remove and discard bay leaves and thyme sprigs. Season with salt and pepper and serve.

Slow Cooker Chickpeas with Kale and Sausage

Chickpeas are a good way to add some substance to a vegetarian dish. They're filling, affordable, and they pair well with an array of herbs and spices. You can try your own blend of flavorings.

2 (15-ounce) cans chickpeas, drained and rinsed

1 large bunch kale, stems removed and leaves chopped

4 (3-ounce) Italian sausages

1 medium yellow onion, peeled and sliced

5 cloves garlic, peeled and smashed

1 (28-ounce) can diced tomatoes

½ cup extra-virgin olive oil

1 teaspoon sea salt

1 teaspoon crushed red pepper flakes

½ cup chopped fresh basil

½ cup grated Romano cheese

1 Place chickpeas, kale, sausages, onion, garlic, tomatoes, and oil in a 4–6-quart slow cooker. Cover and cook on high for 4 hours.

2 Uncover and stir in salt and pepper flakes.

3 Garnish with basil and cheese before serving.

SERVES 4

Per Serving:	
Calories	855
Fat	58g
Sodium	1,948mg
Carbohydrates	51g
Fiber	14g
Sugar	13g
Protein	35g

BASIL

The word "basil" in Greek is *basilikos*, which means "king." In the Mediterranean, there's no doubt that basil is the king of herbs. There are many varieties to be found, so try as many as you can to find your favorite.

Braised Lamb Shanks and Potatoes

SERVES 8

Per Serving:

Calories	518
Fat	14g
Sodium	1,915mg
Carbohydrates	57g
Fiber	5g
Sugar	5g
Protein	36g

AN EASY WAY TO CLEAN A SLOW COOKER

If there is food stuck inside your slow cooker's insert, don't be tempted to soak it in the sink overnight. If your slow cooker insert has an unglazed bottom, it will absorb the water, which may lead to cracking. Instead, place the slow cooker on the counter and use a pitcher to fill the insert with water. Then turn the slow cooker to low and let it cook for a few hours. The heated water will loosen the stuck food and make cleanup easy.

Lamb shanks are tougher than other cuts because the meat is a muscle. However, they become extra tender after a low and slow cooking process.

4 (14-ounce) lamb shanks
¼ cup olive oil
2 large yellow onions, peeled and chopped
3 cloves garlic, peeled and minced
1 medium red bell pepper, seeded and sliced
2 tablespoons tomato paste
1 cup dry red wine
1 cup vegetable stock
3 bay leaves
1 teaspoon smoked paprika
2 teaspoons sea salt
½ teaspoon ground black pepper
6 large russet potatoes, peeled and cut into wedges

1 Spray a 4–6-quart slow cooker with nonstick cooking spray. Add lamb, oil, onions, garlic, bell pepper, tomato paste, wine, stock, bay leaves, paprika, salt, and pepper. Cover and cook on high for 3 hours.
2 Uncover and add potatoes. Cover and cook on high for 1 hour.
3 Remove and discard bay leaves. Serve hot.

Lamb and Artichokes in Lemon Sauce

Lamb is a "free-range, no hormone" meat, and when slow cooked, it's fork-tender and succulent. Most butcher shops carry lamb, and some supermarkets even sell it precut.

2 pounds bone-in leg of lamb or lamb shoulder, cut into large chunks

1½ teaspoons sea salt

½ teaspoon ground black pepper

2 medium yellow onions, peeled and sliced

1 large carrot, peeled and sliced

12 small artichokes, peeled, trimmed, and chokes removed

8 scallions, trimmed and chopped

1 teaspoon sweet paprika

2 teaspoons fresh thyme leaves

2 bay leaves

6 whole peppercorns

3 cups chicken stock

1 large egg

1½ tablespoons lemon juice

2 tablespoons cold water

2 tablespoons cornstarch

½ cup chopped fresh dill

SERVES 6	
Per Serving:	
Calories	379
Fat	21g
Sodium	1,169mg
Carbohydrates	18g
Fiber	6g
Sugar	4g
Protein	32g

1 Season lamb with salt and pepper and place in a 4–6-quart slow cooker. Add onions, carrot, artichokes, scallions, paprika, thyme, bay leaves, peppercorns, and stock. Stir to combine.

2 Cover and cook on high for 6 hours. Remove and discard bay leaves.

3 In a small bowl, combine egg, lemon juice, water, and cornstarch. Whisk until smooth, then uncover slow cooker and stir mixture into contents. Cover and cook for 10 minutes on high or until sauce thickens.

4 Stir in dill and serve.

Slow Cooker Gyro Meatloaf

SERVES 8

Per Serving:

Calories	376
Fat	19g
Sodium	800mg
Carbohydrates	13g
Fiber	1g
Sugar	2g
Protein	35g

Cut this tasty meatloaf into large slices and serve in a bun or pita bread with tzatziki, tomatoes, and onions.

2 pounds 85/15 ground beef

1 medium yellow onion, peeled and grated

3 cloves garlic, peeled and minced

2 large eggs

1 cup bread crumbs

1 teaspoon sweet paprika

1 teaspoon ground allspice

2 teaspoons sea salt

½ teaspoon ground black pepper

2 teaspoons dried Greek oregano

1 Place all ingredients in a large bowl. Use your hands to mix ingredients together. Transfer mixture to a sheet of parchment paper and form into a loaf that will fit into your slow cooker.

2 Use the ends of the parchment to lift meatloaf and place in a 4–6-quart slow cooker. Cover and cook on high for 3 hours.

3 Remove meatloaf from slow cooker and discard any fat remaining in the cooker.

4 Allow to cool for 15 minutes before slicing.

Braciola

Look for steaks that are approximately 1/8" thick, 8"–10" long, and 5" wide to make this Italian dish.

½ teaspoon olive oil

½ cup minced yellow onion

2 cloves garlic, peeled and minced

1 (32-ounce) can diced tomatoes

8 very thin-cut round steaks (1½ pounds total)

8 medium stalks rapini

4 teaspoons dried bread crumbs

4 teaspoons grated Parmesan cheese

1 Place oil, onions, garlic, and tomatoes in a 6-quart oval slow cooker and stir to combine.

2 Place steaks flat on a platter. Sprinkle each with ½ teaspoon bread crumbs and ½ teaspoon cheese. Remove leaves from 1 rapini stalk and discard stalk. Place leaves on one end of a steak. Roll steak lengthwise so that the rapini filling is wrapped tightly. It should look like a spiral. Repeat with remaining rapini and steaks.

3 Place each roll in a single layer on top of the tomato mixture in slow cooker. Cover and cook on low for 1–2 hours until steaks are no longer pink.

4 Serve immediately.

SERVES 8

Per Serving:

Calories	149
Fat	4g
Sodium	185mg
Carbohydrates	7g
Fiber	2g
Sugar	3g
Protein	20g

PROTECT YOUR SLOW COOKER

When the party's over, don't forget to let your slow cooker insert cool before you fill it with dishwater. If it's still hot when you add the water, it could crack. Once it's cooled and you've added water, you might want to let it soak overnight to loosen any hardened foods.

Short Ribs of Beef with Red Wine

Use your favorite dry red wine in this succulent beef dish. Serve it on polenta or mashed potatoes to absorb the rich sauce.

1½ pounds short ribs of beef, excess fat trimmed

1 tablespoon ground cumin

1 teaspoon dried thyme

½ teaspoon onion powder

½ teaspoon garlic powder

½ teaspoon salt

1 teaspoon ground black pepper

2 large red onions, peeled and chopped

12 large plum tomatoes, chopped

1 cup dry red wine

4 cups vegetable broth

2 tablespoons minced parsley

1 Season ribs with cumin, thyme, onion powder, garlic powder, salt, and pepper. Place ribs in a 4–6-quart slow cooker. Add onions, tomatoes, wine, and broth.

2 Cover and cook on low for 6–8 hours. If you want the sauce to thicken, uncover and cook on high for 15 minutes.

3 Garnish with parsley and serve hot.

SERVES 6

Per Serving:

Calories	159
Fat	6g
Sodium	655mg
Carbohydrates	9g
Fiber	2g
Sugar	4g
Protein	11g

BE PATIENT—DON'T PEEK

Keeping the lid on is the whole trick to slow cooking. The steam has to build up inside the cooker, and it takes time (about 15 minutes) to do so. Each time you lift the lid, the steam escapes, adding another 15 minutes to cooking time.

Beef Kapama with Eggplant

SERVES 8

Per Serving:

Calories	345
Fat	16g
Sodium	754mg
Carbohydrates	22g
Fiber	7g
Sugar	11g
Protein	27g

There are many dishes in Greek and Eastern Mediterranean cuisine with the title "kapama." It simply refers to dishes that are stews. Adding eggplant to beef was a way to stretch a meal to feed large families. Eggplant is a great meat substitute and will take on the flavors of whatever you pair with it.

2 pounds boneless beef chuck or short ribs, cut into large cubes

2 medium yellow onions, peeled and diced

6 cloves garlic, peeled and minced

2 cups puréed tomatoes

2 tablespoons tomato paste

½ cup red wine

3 bay leaves

6 whole allspice berries

2 teaspoons sea salt, divided

1 teaspoon ground black pepper, divided

3 medium eggplants, trimmed and cut into large cubes

½ cup minced fresh parsley

1 Place beef, onions, garlic, puréed tomatoes, tomato paste, wine, bay leaves, allspice berries, 1 teaspoon salt, and ½ teaspoon pepper in a 4–6-quart slow cooker. Add enough water to almost cover beef. Cover and cook on low for 5–6 hours until beef is tender.

2 Uncover and add eggplant and remaining 1 teaspoon salt and ½ teaspoon pepper. Cover and cook on high for 10 minutes.

3 Remove and discard bay leaves. Top with parsley before serving.

CHAPTER 6

Pressure Cooker and Instant Pot® Dishes

Fassoulada (Greek White Bean Soup)

SERVES 8

Per Serving:

Calories	290
Fat	7g
Sodium	403mg
Carbohydrates	44g
Fiber	17g
Sugar	5g
Protein	15g

This bean soup is a national dish in Greece—every home cook makes it. Although there are many regional twists to this hearty soup, the approach is the same—simple.

4 cups water

1 pound dried white kidney beans, soaked overnight, drained, and rinsed

2 medium carrots, peeled and sliced

2 medium yellow onions, peeled and diced

2 stalks celery, trimmed and thinly sliced

1 medium parsnip, peeled and thinly sliced

1 cup tomato sauce

1 tablespoon dried rosemary

1 tablespoon dried thyme

3 bay leaves

4 tablespoons minced fresh parsley

¼ cup olive oil

4 cloves garlic, peeled and smashed

¾ teaspoon salt

½ teaspoon ground black pepper

1 Place water, beans, carrots, onions, celery, parsnip, tomato sauce, rosemary, thyme, bay leaves, parsley, oil, and garlic in an Instant Pot®.

2 Close lid, press the Bean button, and cook for the default time of 30 minutes. When the timer beeps, let pressure release naturally, about 20 minutes. Open lid, remove and discard bay leaves, and season with salt and pepper. Serve hot.

Fakes (Greek Lentil Soup)

This filling soup is eaten all over Greece. It uses humble ingredients and is full of protein and iron. Make it part of your regular rotation.

1 pound dried brown lentils, drained and rinsed

2 cups water

2 medium yellow onions, peeled and diced

1 large carrot, peeled, halved lengthwise, and sliced

1 medium red bell pepper, seeded and diced

3 cloves garlic, peeled and smashed

2 tablespoons extra-virgin olive oil

1 (15-ounce) can crushed tomatoes

3 bay leaves

1 tablespoon paprika

¾ teaspoon salt

2 tablespoons dried oregano

5 cloves garlic, peeled and minced

2 tablespoons red wine vinegar

SERVES 6	
Per Serving:	
Calories	367
Fat	6g
Sodium	151mg
Carbohydrates	61g
Fiber	12g
Sugar	8g
Protein	21g

1 Add lentils, water, onions, carrot, bell pepper, smashed garlic, oil, tomatoes, bay leaves, paprika, and salt to an Instant Pot® and stir well.

2 Close lid, press the Manual or Pressure Cook button, and adjust time to 20 minutes. When the timer beeps, quick-release the pressure until the float valve drops. Open lid and remove and discard bay leaves. Stir in oregano and minced garlic.

3 Ladle into six bowls and drizzle with vinegar before serving.

Greek-Style Black-Eyed Pea Soup

Don't drain the tomatoes before adding them to the soup. The liquid in the can adds a tremendous amount of tomato flavor to the broth.

2 tablespoons olive oil

2 stalks celery, trimmed and chopped

1 medium yellow onion, peeled and chopped

2 cloves garlic, peeled and minced

2 tablespoons chopped fresh oregano

1 teaspoon fresh thyme leaves

1 pound dried black-eyed peas, soaked overnight, drained, and rinsed

¼ teaspoon salt

1 teaspoon ground black pepper

4 cups water

1 (14.5-ounce) can diced tomatoes

1 Press the Sauté button on an Instant Pot® and heat oil. Add celery and onion and cook until just tender, about 5 minutes. Add garlic, oregano, and thyme and cook until fragrant, about 30 seconds. Press the Cancel button.

2 Add black-eyed peas, salt, pepper, water, and tomatoes to the Instant Pot® and stir well. Close lid, press the Manual or Pressure Cook button, and adjust time to 20 minutes. When the timer beeps, let pressure release naturally, about 20 minutes.

3 Open lid and stir well. Serve hot.

Zesty Cabbage Soup

Eliminate the chili pepper in this recipe if you don't like spicy food.

2 tablespoons extra-virgin olive oil

3 medium yellow onions, peeled and chopped

1 large carrot, peeled, quartered, and sliced

1 stalk celery, trimmed and chopped

3 bay leaves

1 teaspoon smoked paprika

3 cups sliced white cabbage

1 teaspoon fresh thyme leaves

3 cloves garlic, peeled and minced

½ cup chopped roasted red bell pepper

1 (15-ounce) can white navy beans, drained and rinsed

1½ cups vegetable juice drink

7 cups vegetable stock

1 small dried chili pepper

2 medium zucchini, trimmed, halved lengthwise, and thinly sliced

1 teaspoon salt

½ teaspoon ground black pepper

1 Press the Sauté button on an Instant Pot® and heat oil. Add onions, carrot, celery, and bay leaves. Cook for 7–10 minutes or until vegetables are soft.

2 Add paprika, cabbage, thyme, garlic, roasted pepper, and beans. Stir to combine and cook for 2 minutes. Add vegetable drink, stock, and chili pepper. Press the Cancel button.

3 Close lid, press the Soup button, and cook for the default time of 20 minutes. When the timer beeps, quick-release the pressure until the float valve drops and open lid.

4 Remove and discard bay leaves. Add zucchini, close lid, and let stand on the Keep Warm setting for 15 minutes. Season with salt and black pepper. Serve hot.

SERVES 8

Per Serving:

Calories	94
Fat	4g
Sodium	894mg
Carbohydrates	14g
Fiber	2g
Sugar	9g
Protein	2g

CABBAGE

Cabbage is an under-rated vegetable that should be included in more meals. It's a good source of fiber and vitamin C. It's also a great colon cleanser and a detoxifier for the entire body.

Red Lentil and Carrot Soup

SERVES 6

Per Serving:

Calories	317
Fat	6g
Sodium	145mg
Carbohydrates	52g
Fiber	9g
Sugar	5g
Protein	17g

Everyone is familiar with the orange carrot, but did you know that carrots come in a variety of colors, such as white, purple, red, and yellow? If you can get your hands on any of these fancy carrots, use them to make this soup.

2 tablespoons olive oil

4 medium carrots, peeled and sliced

1 medium yellow onion, peeled and chopped

1 stalk celery, trimmed and chopped

1 tablespoon grated fresh ginger

2 cloves garlic, peeled and minced

¼ teaspoon ground allspice

½ teaspoon ground black pepper

¼ teaspoon salt

2 cups dried red lentils, drained and rinsed

6 cups water

1 tablespoon minced parsley

1 Press the Sauté button on an Instant Pot® and heat oil. Add carrots, onion, and celery. Sauté 5 minutes. Add ginger, garlic, allspice, pepper, and salt and cook for 30 seconds. Press the Cancel button.

2 Stir in lentils and water. Close lid, press the Manual or Pressure Cook button, and adjust time to 12 minutes. When the timer beeps, let pressure release naturally, about 15 minutes. Open lid and stir well. Sprinkle with parsley before serving.

Heirloom Tomato Basil Soup

SERVES 4

Per Serving:

Calories	317
Fat	27g
Sodium	382mg
Carbohydrates	16g
Fiber	4g
Sugar	9g
Protein	8g

WHERE DO HEIRLOOM TOMATOES COME FROM?

Heirloom tomatoes are grown from seeds harvested from older varieties that were popular in the past. They're easy to spot in the store, because they look so different from today's uniform red spheres. Heirlooms can be sweet or slightly tart, and they come in a variety of colors and shapes. In late summer, there's nothing better than a platter of sliced heirloom tomatoes, showcasing a riot of color!

If you love tomato soup, this dish is going to make your day. To make it even better, top the soup with grilled cheese croutons. Make a grilled cheese sandwich as you normally would and then cut the sandwich into little squares. Float these glorious croutons atop your soup and enjoy this new twist on an old classic.

1 tablespoon olive oil

1 small yellow onion, peeled and diced

1 stalk celery, trimmed and sliced

8 medium heirloom tomatoes, seeded and quartered

¼ cup julienned fresh basil

½ teaspoon salt

3 cups low-sodium chicken broth

1 cup heavy cream

1 teaspoon ground black pepper

1 Press the Sauté button on an Instant Pot® and heat oil. Add onion and celery and cook until translucent, about 5 minutes. Add tomatoes and cook for 3 minutes or until tomatoes are tender and start to break down. Add basil, salt, and broth. Press the Cancel button.

2 Close lid, press the Manual or Pressure Cook button, and adjust time to 7 minutes. When the timer beeps, quick-release the pressure until the float valve drops and then open lid.

3 Add cream and pepper. Purée soup with an immersion blender or in batches in a blender. Ladle into four bowls and serve warm.

Chickpea Soup

Looking to cut your meat intake? Chickpeas are a great alternative.
They're affordable, filling, and a good source of protein.

2 cups dried chickpeas

1 teaspoon baking soda

1 medium lemon

2 tablespoons extra-virgin olive oil

2 cups diced yellow onion

1 medium carrot, peeled and finely diced

1 stalk celery, trimmed and finely diced

4 cloves garlic, peeled and minced

8 cups vegetable stock

¼ cup chopped fresh parsley

3 bay leaves

1 teaspoon paprika

½ teaspoon dried oregano

¾ teaspoon salt

½ teaspoon ground black pepper

SERVES 6

Per Serving:

Calories	340
Fat	9g
Sodium	1,404mg
Carbohydrates	52g
Fiber	10g
Sugar	12g
Protein	15g

1. Place chickpeas in a large bowl. Add baking soda and enough water to cover. Soak overnight, then drain and rinse chickpeas.
2. Cut lemon in half. Slice one half and cut the other half into six wedges.
3. Press the Sauté button on an Instant Pot® and heat oil. Sauté onion, carrot, and celery for 5–7 minutes until softened. Stir in garlic and sauté 1 minute. Add stock, chickpeas, lemon slices, parsley, bay leaves, and paprika and bring just to a boil. Press the Cancel button.
4. Close lid, press the Manual or Pressure Cook button, and adjust time to 15 minutes. When the timer beeps, quick-release the pressure until the float valve drops. Press the Cancel button and open lid.
5. Remove and discard bay leaves and lemon slices and season with oregano, salt, and pepper.
6. Serve immediately with lemon wedges.

Artichoke Soup

SERVES 8

Per Serving:

Calories	342
Fat	5g
Sodium	1,332mg
Carbohydrates	68g
Fiber	19g
Sugar	9g
Protein	16g

ARTICHOKES

Artichokes are enjoyed around the globe and come in a number of varieties, including green, purple, and white. When working with artichokes, it's a good idea to rub their cut surfaces with lemon to avoid browning. Artichokes should be firm, with closely fitted leaves and a plump stem.

Artichokes are part of the thistle family and grow wild in the Mediterranean. Rinse artichokes thoroughly under running water, making sure water runs between leaves to flush out any debris.

18 large artichokes, peeled, trimmed, halved, and chokes removed

1 medium lemon, halved

6 tablespoons lemon juice, divided

2 tablespoons extra-virgin olive oil

6 medium leeks, trimmed, cut lengthwise, and sliced

¾ teaspoons salt, divided

½ teaspoon ground black pepper, divided

3 large russet potatoes, peeled and quartered

10 cups vegetable stock

½ cup plain low-fat Greek yogurt

½ cup chopped fresh chives

1 Rub each artichoke half with lemon. In a large bowl, combine artichokes, enough water to cover them, and 3 tablespoons lemon juice. Set aside.

2 Press the Sauté button on an Instant Pot® and heat oil. Add leeks, ½ teaspoon salt, and ¼ teaspoon pepper. Cook for 10 minutes or until leeks are softened.

3 Drain artichokes and add to leeks along with potatoes and stock. Add remaining ¼ teaspoon each salt and pepper.

4 Press the Cancel button, close lid, press the Soup button, and cook for the default time of 20 minutes. When the timer beeps, let pressure release naturally, about 25 minutes. Press the Cancel button and open lid.

5 Purée soup in an immersion blender or in batches in a blender until smooth. Stir in remaining 3 tablespoons lemon juice.

6 Serve soup with a dollop of yogurt and a sprinkle of chives.

Spaghetti Squash with Mushrooms

Mushrooms have a hearty flavor and a satisfying meaty texture. They are also a great source of plant-based protein and fiber, which makes you feel satisfied longer. Any mushrooms will work in this recipe, so use the ones you like best.

1 cup water

1 (3-pound) spaghetti squash, sliced in half lengthwise and seeded

2 tablespoons olive oil

4 cups sliced button mushrooms

2 cloves garlic, peeled and minced

1 tablespoon chopped fresh oregano

1 tablespoon chopped fresh basil

¼ teaspoon crushed red pepper flakes

1 cup marinara sauce

½ cup shredded Parmesan cheese

SERVES 4

Per Serving:

Calories	232
Fat	12g
Sodium	505mg
Carbohydrates	26g
Fiber	5g
Sugar	12g
Protein	9g

1 Place the rack in an Instant Pot®, add water, and place squash on rack. Close lid, press the Manual or Pressure Cook button, and adjust time to 7 minutes.

2 When the timer beeps, quick-release the pressure until the float valve drops. Press the Cancel button and open lid. Carefully remove squash from pot and set aside to cool for 10 minutes, then take a fork and shred flesh into a medium bowl.

3 Wash and dry pot. Press the Sauté button and heat oil. Add mushrooms and cook until tender and any juices have evaporated, about 8 minutes. Add garlic and cook until fragrant, about 30 seconds.

4 Add squash to pot and toss to mix. Add oregano, basil, pepper flakes, and marinara sauce and toss to coat. Press the Cancel button. Top with cheese and close the lid. Let stand for 5 minutes until cheese melts. Serve hot.

Butternut Squash Soup

The spices in this recipe add lots of depth and warmth to a soup that will stick to your ribs on a cold night.

1 (3-pound) whole butternut squash, peeled, seeded, and cut into chunks

1½ cups diced yellow onion

2 cloves garlic, peeled and chopped

¼ cup olive oil

8 cups chicken or vegetable stock

2 teaspoons ground fennel seed

1½ teaspoons sea salt

½ teaspoon ground black pepper

½ cup crumbled feta cheese

1 tablespoon plain whole-milk Greek yogurt

1. Place squash, onion, garlic, oil, stock, fennel seed, salt, and pepper in a pressure cooker and lock the lid.
2. Bring to high pressure over high heat; maintain for 12 minutes. Remove from heat and allow pressure to release naturally, about 20 minutes.
3. Open lid and allow soup to cool for 5 minutes. Use a handheld blender to purée soup until smooth.
4. In a small bowl, mash cheese and stir in yogurt.
5. Serve soup with a dollop of cheese mixture on top.

SERVES 8

Per Serving:

Calories	177
Fat	9g
Sodium	1,185mg
Carbohydrates	22g
Fiber	4g
Sugar	5g
Protein	4g

Barley Risotto with Mushrooms

SERVES 6

Per Serving:

Calories	260
Fat	6g
Sodium	696mg
Carbohydrates	44g
Fiber	8g
Sugar	3g
Protein	8g

BARLEY

Barley is filling and loaded with fiber, and it can help to keep your blood sugar level steady. It's also a good source of phosphorus, potassium and folate. Pearl (or pearled) barley is the most common form of barley. It's not a whole grain, because the outer husk and the bran layers have been removed. Hulled barley is a whole grain; only the outer husk has been removed. You can use hulled barley in recipes that call for pearl barley, but it will need more time to cook.

Barley is a great alternative to rice, and this version of risotto with mushrooms may be your new go-to dish. Making risotto in the Instant Pot® means you don't have to add stock and stir constantly as it cooks. It's a great weeknight option.

2 tablespoons extra-virgin olive oil

1 large yellow onion, peeled and diced

1 clove garlic, peeled and minced

2 cups sliced white mushrooms

2 bay leaves

¼ teaspoon fresh thyme leaves

1½ cups pearl barley, rinsed and drained

4 cups vegetable stock

¼ cup dry white wine

2 cups water

½ teaspoon salt

¼ teaspoon ground black pepper

¼ cup grated Parmesan cheese

1 Press the Sauté button on an Instant Pot® and heat oil. Add onion and sauté for 5 minutes. Add garlic and cook for 30 seconds. Stir in mushrooms, bay leaves, and thyme and sauté for 5 minutes. Stir in barley, stock, wine, water, salt, and pepper. Press the Cancel button.

2 Close lid, press the Manual or Pressure Cook button, and adjust time to 18 minutes. When the timer beeps, quick-release the pressure until the float valve drops and open the lid.

3 Drain off excess liquid, leaving just enough so that risotto is slightly soupy. Press the Cancel button, then press the Sauté button and cook until thickened, about 5 minutes. Remove and discard bay leaves. Stir in cheese and serve immediately.

Eggplant with Sour Trahana

Trahana is a dried food made with wheat and yogurt or fermented milk. It's been a part of Greek cuisine for centuries. Lactic acid gives trahana its characteristic sour taste and contributes to its long-lasting quality. It makes a lovely, thick soup. If you can't find tarhana, Israeli couscous makes a good substitute.

½ cup extra-virgin olive oil, divided

2 medium Italian eggplants, trimmed, cut in half lengthwise, each half cut into 3 long wedges

2 cups sliced yellow onion

3 cloves garlic, peeled and minced

2 cups tomato purée

1 cup minced fresh parsley

2 teaspoons sea salt

½ teaspoon ground black pepper

8 ounces (about 1 cup) sour trahana

1 cup crumbled feta cheese

1 Press the Sauté button on an Instant Pot® and heat ¼ cup oil. Brown half the eggplant wedges on all sides, 3–4 minutes per side. Drain on a paper towel–lined plate. Repeat with the remaining ¼ cup oil and eggplant. Press the Cancel button.

2 Return eggplant to Instant Pot® and add onion, garlic, tomato purée, parsley, salt, and pepper. Close lid, press the Slow Cook button, set steam release to Venting, and adjust time to 90 minutes.

3 When the timer beeps, open the lid and add trahana. If there is not enough liquid to cover trahana, add hot water to cover. Close lid, set steam release to Venting, and adjust time to 45 minutes.

4 Open the lid and transfer to a platter or four plates and top with cheese. Serve hot.

SERVES 4

Per Serving:

Calories	673
Fat	36g
Sodium	1,779mg
Carbohydrates	74g
Fiber	13g
Sugar	17g
Protein	18g

EGGPLANT SEASON

Eating eggplant when in season offers the best results. In-season eggplant contains little to no seeds, and therefore no bitterness. You can even skip pre-salting or pre-soaking. When eggplant is not in season, Japanese eggplants are a good alternative. They're smaller and they have a natural sweetness.

Pressure Cooker Gigantes Beans

MEDITERRANEAN BEANS

Beans and legumes figure prominently in Mediterranean cuisine; they've been consumed since ancient times in the region. A healthy, inexpensive staple, they're available year-round. If you want to skip the pre-soak step, use cans of rinsed beans. No one will know!

Gigantes *means "giant" in Greek. These oversized, creamy beans are also called "elephant beans." If you can't find gigantes, use large lima beans.*

¼ cup extra-virgin olive oil

1 cup diced yellow onion

1 cup diced carrot

½ cup diced celery

2 cloves garlic, peeled and minced

1 pound dried gigantes beans or large lima beans, soaked overnight in water to cover

¼ cup tomato purée

1 tablespoon tomato paste

½ teaspoon ground allspice

3 bay leaves

1½ teaspoons sea salt

½ teaspoon ground black pepper

3 cups water

1 Heat oil in a pressure cooker over medium heat. Add onion, carrot, celery, and garlic and sauté for 5–6 minutes until translucent.

2 Drain beans and add to pressure cooker. Stir in tomato purée, tomato paste, allspice, bay leaves, salt, pepper, and water. Lock the lid into place. Bring to high pressure; maintain for 45 minutes.

3 Remove from heat and allow pressure to release naturally for 25 minutes. Unlock valve to release any remaining pressure.

4 Uncover; remove and discard bay leaves before serving.

Potatoes Provençal

Provence is the southernmost area of France on the Mediterranean Sea. The cuisine of this region has more in common with the other Southern Mediterranean countries than it does with Northern France.

¼ cup extra-virgin olive oil

2 pounds russet potatoes, peeled and cut into 1" pieces

1 cup sliced yellow onion

1 cup diced tomato

3 cloves garlic, peeled and minced

1 medium bell pepper, seeded and sliced

1 teaspoon fresh thyme leaves

2 bay leaves

1 teaspoon sea salt

½ teaspoon ground black pepper

¾ cup water

20 Kalamata olives

SERVES 6	
Per Serving:	
Calories	257
Fat	13g
Sodium	600mg
Carbohydrates	34g
Fiber	3g
Sugar	4g
Protein	4g

1 Heat oil in a pressure cooker over medium-high heat. Sauté potatoes for 5 minutes. Add onion and tomato and sauté for 5 minutes.

2 Stir in garlic, bell pepper, thyme, bay leaves, salt, black pepper, and water. Lock the lid into place. Bring to high pressure; maintain for 13 minutes. Remove from heat and allow pressure to release naturally, about 20 minutes. Open lid.

3 Remove and discard bay leaves. Add olives and serve immediately.

Pearl Couscous Salad

Also known as Israeli couscous, large-grained pearl couscous is perfect for this refreshing side salad because it adds more substance than its smaller counterpart. The acidity and sweetness of the orange juice combined with the freshness of the cucumber, bell pepper, and tomatoes will keep you coming back for more.

3 tablespoons olive oil, divided

1 cup pearl couscous

1 cup water

1 cup orange juice

1 small cucumber, seeded and diced

1 small yellow bell pepper, seeded and diced

2 small Roma tomatoes, diced

¼ cup slivered almonds

¼ cup chopped fresh mint

2 tablespoons lemon juice

1 teaspoon grated lemon zest

¼ cup crumbled feta cheese

¼ teaspoon fine sea salt

1 teaspoon smoked paprika

1 teaspoon garlic powder

1 Press the Sauté button on an Instant Pot® and heat 1 tablespoon oil. Add couscous and cook for 2–4 minutes until couscous is slightly browned. Add water and orange juice. Press the Cancel button.

2 Close lid, press the Manual or Pressure Cook button, and adjust time to 5 minutes. When the timer beeps, let pressure release naturally for 5 minutes. Quick-release any remaining pressure until the float valve drops and open lid. Drain any liquid and set aside to cool for 20 minutes.

3 Combine remaining 2 tablespoons oil, cucumber, bell pepper, tomatoes, almonds, mint, lemon juice, lemon zest, cheese, salt, paprika, and garlic powder in a medium bowl. Add couscous and toss ingredients together. Cover and refrigerate overnight before serving.

Pasta Primavera

PASTA PRIMAVERA

You may think pasta primavera is an Italian invention, but the dish actually originated in the United States and Canada and was first served in the mid-1970s in New York. Its exact origins are murky, with multiple people laying claim to inventing the dish, but it exploded in popularity after the recipe was printed in *The New York Times*. If you are looking to enjoy more plant-based meals, this recipe is sure to become a favorite.

This easy pasta dish is perfect for a mild spring day or anytime you want something light and refreshing for lunch or dinner. While the vegetables in this recipe are ideal for springtime, it can be adapted to use whatever vegetables are in season. Try a different primavera for all four seasons.

1 pound bow tie pasta

4 cups water

2 tablespoons olive oil, divided

1½ cups chopped summer squash

1½ cups chopped zucchini

3 cups chopped broccoli

½ cup sun-dried tomatoes

2 cloves garlic, peeled and chopped

1 cup white wine

2 tablespoons cold unsalted butter

½ teaspoon salt

¾ teaspoon ground black pepper

¼ cup chopped fresh basil

1 Place pasta, water, and 1 tablespoon oil in an Instant Pot®. Close lid, press the Manual or Pressure Cook button, and adjust time to 4 minutes. When the timer beeps, quick-release the pressure until the float valve drops. Press the Cancel button and open the lid. Drain pasta and set aside.

2 Wash and dry pot. Press the Sauté button and heat remaining 1 tablespoon oil. Add squash, zucchini, broccoli, and sun-dried tomatoes and cook until very tender, about 10 minutes. Add garlic and wine. Allow wine to reduce for 2–3 minutes.

3 Add butter to pot, stirring constantly to create an emulsion. Season with salt and pepper.

4 Pour sauce and vegetables over pasta and stir to coat. Top with basil.

Shrimp Risotto

Risotto is a magical dish made with short-grain Arborio rice that releases starch to make a creamy sauce. Cooking risotto on the stove can take almost an hour from start to finish. With this recipe, you work for a few minutes, and the Instant Pot® does the rest.

4 tablespoons olive oil, divided

1 medium yellow onion, peeled and chopped

1 clove garlic, peeled and minced

1 teaspoon fresh thyme leaves

1½ cups Arborio rice

½ cup white wine

4 cups low-sodium chicken broth

1 pound medium shrimp, peeled and deveined

½ teaspoon ground black pepper

½ cup grated Parmesan cheese

1 Press the Sauté button on an Instant Pot® and heat 2 tablespoons oil. Add onion and cook until tender, about 3 minutes. Add garlic and thyme and cook for 30 seconds. Add rice and cook, stirring so each grain is coated in oil, for 3 minutes.

2 Add wine to the Instant Pot® and cook, stirring constantly, until it is almost completely evaporated, about 2 minutes. Add broth and bring to a simmer, stirring constantly, about 3 minutes.

3 Press the Cancel button. Close lid, press the Manual or Pressure Cook button, and adjust time to 6 minutes. When the timer beeps, let pressure release naturally for 15 minutes, then quick-release the remaining pressure until the float valve drops. Press the Cancel button and open lid.

4 Stir in shrimp and pepper. Press the Sauté button and cook until shrimp are pink, opaque, and curled into a *C* shape, about 4 minutes. Divide risotto among six bowls and top with cheese and remaining 2 tablespoons oil. Serve immediately.

SERVES 6

Per Serving:

Calories	229
Fat	12g
Sodium	543mg
Carbohydrates	13g
Fiber	1g
Sugar	1g
Protein	14g

SHRIMP: A CONVENIENCE FOOD

There was a time when shrimp was exotic and somewhat intimidating to cook with, but today all that has changed. Shrimp in a variety of sizes are plentiful due to the addition of farm-raised shrimp to the market. You can easily find shrimp already peeled and deveined so it's ready to cook. They take no more than 5 minutes to cook, so you should always have a bag of frozen shrimp in your freezer.

Fish with Spinach and Rice

SERVES 4

Per Serving:

Calories	361
Fat	11g
Sodium	365mg
Carbohydrates	41g
Fiber	1g
Sugar	0g
Protein	22g

This is a super-easy weeknight dish, with everything cooked in one pot at the same time. If you prefer, you can replace the whitefish with salmon.

1 cup water

1 cup white rice

3 tablespoons extra-virgin olive oil, divided

4 (4-ounce) cod or other whitefish fillets

½ teaspoon salt

½ teaspoon ground black pepper

2 cups baby spinach

4 lemon wedges

1 Add water, rice, and 1 tablespoon oil to an Instant Pot® and stir well. Place the rack and steamer basket inside the pot.

2 Season fish with salt and pepper. Measure four pieces of foil large enough to wrap around fish fillets. Lay spinach on foil, top with fish, drizzle with the remaining 2 tablespoons oil, and squeeze juice from lemon wedges. Carefully wrap loosely in foil, making sure to seal seams well.

3 Place foil packets in steamer basket. Close lid, press the Steam button, and adjust time to 5 minutes.

4 When the timer beeps, quick-release the pressure until the float valve drops. Press the Cancel button and open lid. Carefully remove packets and set aside. Divide rice between four bowls. Open packets and place fish with spinach on rice. Serve hot.

Cioppino

This version of cioppino (an Italian fish stew) uses only shellfish, but you can add cubed whitefish if you have some on hand. Just add it with the shellfish and simmer until it is opaque and flakes when gently pressed with a fork. Don't forget the crusty bread!

3 tablespoons olive oil

1 medium yellow onion, peeled and chopped

1 medium red bell pepper, seeded and chopped

2 cloves garlic, peeled and minced

1 (28-ounce) can crushed tomatoes

1 cup red wine

1 cup seafood stock

1 tablespoon lemon juice

1 bay leaf

¼ cup chopped fresh basil

½ teaspoon ground black pepper

1 pound fresh mussels, scrubbed and beards removed

1 pound large shrimp, peeled and deveined

1 pound fresh clams, scrubbed

1 Press the Sauté button on an Instant Pot® and heat oil. Add onion and bell pepper. Cook until just tender, about 3 minutes. Add garlic and cook until fragrant, about 30 seconds. Add tomatoes, wine, stock, lemon juice, bay leaf, basil, and black pepper. Stir well. Press the Cancel button.

2 Close lid, press the Manual or Pressure Cook button, and adjust time to 5 minutes. When the timer beeps, quick-release the pressure until the float valve drops. Press the Cancel button and open lid. Remove and discard bay leaf. Add mussels, shrimp, and clams. Press the Sauté button and cook until shrimp are pink and shellfish have opened, about 3 minutes. Discard any mussels that haven't opened. Serve hot.

SERVES 6

Per Serving:

Calories	269
Fat	9g
Sodium	1,115mg
Carbohydrates	17g
Fiber	3g
Sugar	8g
Protein	23g

AN ITALIAN-AMERICAN FAVORITE

If you've visited the San Francisco area, chances are you've eaten a bowl of cioppino. Italian immigrants in the area made the dish famous, using a variety of local seafood. It's a wonderful example of old-world technique being applied to new-world ingredients.

Chicken Breasts Stuffed with Feta and Spinach

This dish looks like a million bucks and could not be easier to make. If you prefer, you can replace the feta with shredded mozzarella or goat cheese. Make sure to wring as much water from the spinach as you can to keep the filling firm.

1 cup chopped frozen spinach, thawed and drained well

½ cup crumbled feta cheese

4 (6-ounce) boneless, skinless chicken breasts

¼ teaspoon salt

¼ teaspoon ground black pepper

2 tablespoons olive oil, divided

1 cup water

1 In a small bowl, combine spinach and cheese. Slice a pocket into each chicken breast along one side. Stuff one-quarter of the spinach and cheese mixture into the pocket of each breast. Season chicken on all sides with salt and pepper. Set aside.

2 Press the Sauté button on an Instant Pot® and heat 1 tablespoon oil. Add two chicken breasts and brown on both sides, about 3 minutes per side. Transfer to a plate and repeat with remaining 1 tablespoon oil and chicken. Press the Cancel button.

3 Add water to pot and place the rack inside. Place chicken breasts on rack. Close lid, press the Manual or Pressure Cook button, and adjust time to 8 minutes.

4 When the timer beeps, quick-release the pressure until the float valve drops. Press the Cancel button and open lid. Transfer chicken to a serving platter. Serve hot.

Basque Chicken

The Basque region straddles Northern Spain and Southern France. Chicken with peppers and ham is a popular Basque comfort food dish.

4 (10-ounce) chicken leg quarters

1 teaspoon sea salt

½ teaspoon ground black pepper

2 tablespoons olive oil

1 cup diced yellow onion

5 cloves garlic, peeled and smashed

1 cup sliced red bell pepper

½ cup diced ham

1 cup tomato sauce

¼ cup white wine

1 teaspoon grated orange zest

1 cup water

½ cup sliced black olives

½ cup chopped fresh parsley

SERVES 4	
Per Serving:	
Calories	462
Fat	28g
Sodium	1,112mg
Carbohydrates	12g
Fiber	3g
Sugar	6g
Protein	37g

1   Separate chicken quarters into drumsticks and thigh pieces. Score the skin of each piece with a sharp knife. Season both sides with salt and black pepper.

2   Heat oil in a pressure cooker over medium-high heat. Cook chicken pieces in hot oil until browned, about 3 minutes per side.

3   Add onion, garlic, bell pepper, ham, tomato sauce, wine, orange zest, and water. Stir to combine. Bring to a boil, then lock the lid into place. Bring to high pressure; maintain for 15 minutes. Remove from heat and allow pressure to release naturally, about 20 minutes. Open lid.

4   Garnish with olives and parsley and serve.

Kale, Chickpea, and Chicken Stew

Stirring in a little tahini at the end of cooking adds a subtle richness to this stew.

2 tablespoons olive oil

2 large red bell peppers, seeded and chopped

1 medium yellow onion, peeled and chopped

4 cups chopped kale

2 cloves garlic, peeled and minced

3 medium tomatoes, seeded and chopped

2 sprigs fresh thyme

1 pound boneless, skinless chicken breast, cut into 1" pieces

2 (15-ounce) cans chickpeas, drained and rinsed

2 cups low-sodium chicken broth

½ cup tahini

¼ cup chopped fresh parsley

SERVES 8	
Per Serving:	
Calories	326
Fat	16g
Sodium	192mg
Carbohydrates	26g
Fiber	7g
Sugar	6g
Protein	21g

1 Press the Sauté button on an Instant Pot® and heat oil. Add bell peppers and onion and sauté 5 minutes. Add kale and cook until just wilted, about 2 minutes. Add garlic and cook until fragrant, about 30 seconds. Add tomatoes and thyme. Press the Cancel button.

2 Add chicken, chickpeas, and broth. Stir well, then close lid, press the Manual or Pressure Cook button, and adjust time to 5 minutes.

3 When the timer beeps, let pressure release naturally for 15 minutes, then quick-release any remaining pressure until the float valve drops. Open lid, remove thyme sprigs, and stir in tahini. Sprinkle with parsley and serve hot.

Chicken and Orzo Soup

This soup is simple to make, super-comforting, and very filling.

1 pound boneless, skinless chicken breast

3 stalks celery, trimmed and sliced

2 medium carrots, peeled and chopped

1 medium yellow onion, peeled and chopped

2 cups baby spinach

1 clove garlic, peeled and minced

1 bay leaf

2 sprigs fresh sage

2 sprigs fresh thyme

¼ teaspoon ground black pepper

4 cups low-sodium chicken broth

1 cup orzo

1 Place all ingredients except orzo in an Instant Pot®. Close lid and press the Soup button and cook for the default time of 20 minutes. When the timer beeps, quick-release the pressure until the float valve drops. Press the Cancel button and open lid.

2 Use tongs or a slotted spoon to transfer chicken to a cutting board. Carefully shred meat, then return to pot. Remove and discard sage sprigs, thyme sprigs, and bay leaf.

3 Stir in orzo. Close lid, press the Manual or Pressure Cook button, and adjust time to 4 minutes. When the timer beeps, quick-release the pressure until the float valve drops. Press the Cancel button and open lid. Serve hot.

Lentils with Vegetables and Sausage

Lentils and Italian sausage are wonderful together.
The mix of vegetables packs the dish with lots of flavor.

1 cup extra-virgin olive oil

1¼ cups dried brown lentils, rinsed

½ cup diced carrot

½ cup diced turnip

2 (3-ounce) sweet Italian sausages, sliced into 1" pieces

2 bay leaves

3 sprigs fresh thyme

1 teaspoon sweet paprika

1¼ teaspoons sea salt

½ teaspoon ground black pepper

1 Place oil, lentils, carrot, turnip, sausages, bay leaves, thyme, and paprika in a pressure cooker. Heat uncovered over medium-high heat for 3 minutes.

2 Lock the lid into place. Bring to high pressure over medium heat; reduce heat to medium-low and maintain pressure for 20 minutes. Remove from heat and quick-release the pressure.

3 Uncover; remove and discard bay leaves and thyme sprigs. Season with salt and pepper. Let rest for 5 minutes before serving.

SERVES 6

Per Serving:

Calories	566
Fat	44g
Sodium	713mg
Carbohydrates	29g
Fiber	5g
Sugar	2g
Protein	16g

CASSOULET

This dish is inspired by French cassoulet, which is traditionally made with beans and a variety of meats. Using only sausage reduces the cooking time, and lentils are cooked in a fraction of the time needed for white beans.

Cretan Wedding Rice

The food at Greek weddings are an integral part of the celebration and this dish is traditionally served at weddings on the island of Crete. While the ingredients are few, the lamb stock and creamy dollop of yogurt make this a tremendous rice dish.

SERVES 8

Per Serving:

Calories	438
Fat	22g
Sodium	645mg
Carbohydrates	33g
Fiber	1g
Sugar	3g
Protein	25g

LEAN, MILD GOAT MEAT

Goat is a great alternative to lamb, and you can find it at grocery stores serving Middle Eastern, Eastern Mediterranean, and African communities. It's leaner than lamb and has a milder flavor.

2 pounds bone-in lamb or goat shoulder, cut into chunks

2 teaspoons salt

1 teaspoon ground black pepper

2 tablespoons olive oil

1 cup minced yellow onion

6 cups water

2 cups Arborio or other short-grain rice

4 tablespoons unsalted butter

½ cup lemon juice

1 cup plain whole-milk Greek yogurt

1 Season lamb with salt and pepper and set aside.
2 Heat oil in a pressure cooker over high heat. Sauté onion for 4–5 minutes until translucent. Add lamb and brown on all sides. Stir in water. Lock the lid into place. Bring to high pressure, reduce heat to low, and cook for 40 minutes.
3 Remove from heat and allow pressure to release naturally for 25 minutes. Unlock valve to release any remaining pressure. Open lid.
4 Use a slotted spoon to remove meat and set aside. Increase heat to high and add rice to the pressure cooker. Bring to a boil, reduce heat to low, and simmer for 15 minutes or until rice is tender. If necessary, add more water to the pot.
5 Remove pressure cooker from heat and stir in butter and lemon juice.
6 Top rice with a spoonful of yogurt before serving.

Giouvetsi with Keftedes

Giouvetsi is a baked dish of meat and kritharaki (orzo). This version contains keftedes, sometimes called "Greek meatballs."

1 pound 85/15 ground beef

2 (1-ounce) slices stale bread, soaked in water then squeezed dry

1 large egg

1 medium yellow onion, peeled and grated

3 teaspoons minced garlic, divided

1 teaspoon ground allspice

1 teaspoon dried Greek oregano

1 teaspoon sea salt, divided

¾ teaspoon ground black pepper, divided

6 tablespoons olive oil, divided

1 medium yellow onion, peeled and diced

1 medium green or red bell pepper, seeded and diced

2 cups orzo

1 teaspoon smoked paprika

½ cup tomato passata or tomato sauce

6 cups beef or chicken stock

¾ cup grated Parmesan cheese

SERVES 6	
Per Serving:	
Calories	624
Fat	24g
Sodium	1,686mg
Carbohydrates	61g
Fiber	4g
Sugar	6g
Protein	39g

1 Place ground beef, bread, egg, grated onion, 1 teaspoon garlic, allspice, oregano, ½ teaspoon salt, and ¼ teaspoon black pepper in a large bowl and mix with your hands.

2 Form the mixture into palm-sized meatballs, then gently flatten them to form keftedes patties.

3 Press the Sauté button on an Instant Pot® and heat 4 tablespoons oil. In batches, cook keftedes until browned on both sides, 4–5 minutes per side. Drain on a paper towel–lined plate and set aside.

4 Add the remaining 2 tablespoons oil to the Instant Pot® and sauté diced onion, bell pepper, and remaining 2 teaspoons garlic for 5 minutes. Add orzo and stir to coat. Add paprika, tomato passata, stock, keftedes, and remaining ½ teaspoon each salt and black pepper. Press the Cancel button.

5 Close lid, press the Manual or Pressure Cook button, and adjust time to 4 minutes. When the timer beeps, let pressure release naturally for 5 minutes, then quick-release the remaining steam. Press the Cancel button and open lid.

6 Top with cheese and serve.

Bulgur and Beef–Stuffed Peppers

If you prefer, you can bake these peppers in the oven. Place them in a baking dish, top with the Parmesan cheese, and bake at 350°F for 20 minutes or until the cheese is melted and peppers are tender.

STUFFING PEPPERS

When selecting bell peppers for a stuffed pepper recipe, make sure they are firm and unblemished. If the skin is wrinkled or soft, the stuffed pepper will turn out mushy. Make sure the peppers are large enough to hold a good amount of filling. Small peppers are not ideal for a stuffed pepper. And always be sure to cook meat thoroughly before filling the peppers. Peppers will insulate the filling somewhat while cooking, and meat will not come to a safe temperature unless cooked beforehand.

½ cup bulgur wheat

1 cup vegetable broth

2 tablespoons olive oil

1 medium yellow onion, peeled and diced

1 clove garlic, peeled and minced

1 medium Roma tomato, seeded and chopped

1 teaspoon minced fresh rosemary

1 teaspoon fresh thyme leaves

½ teaspoon salt

½ teaspoon ground black pepper

½ pound 90/10 ground beef

4 large red bell peppers, tops and insides removed

½ cup marinara sauce

1 cup water

½ cup grated Parmesan cheese

1 Add bulgur and broth to an Instant Pot® and stir well. Close lid, press the Rice button, adjust pressure to Low, and set time to 12 minutes. When the timer beeps, quick-release the pressure until the float valve drops. Press the Cancel button. Open lid and fluff bulgur with a fork, then transfer to a medium bowl and set aside to cool.

2 Press the Sauté button and heat oil. Add onion and cook until tender, about 5 minutes. Add garlic, tomato, rosemary, thyme, salt, and black pepper and sauté for 1 minute. Add beef and use a large spoon to break up meat into small pieces. Cook until no longer pink, about 5 minutes. Press the Cancel button.

3 Add beef mixture to bulgur and mix well. Divide mixture equally among hollowed-out bell peppers. Top each pepper with marinara sauce.

4 Wash pot, add water, and place the rack in pot. Carefully stand peppers on rack. Close lid, press the Manual or Pressure Cook button, and adjust time to 3 minutes. When the timer beeps, quick-release the pressure until the float valve drops. Open lid and carefully transfer peppers with tongs to plates. Top with cheese and serve immediately.

Giouvarlakia Soup

This hearty soup is a one pot meal. The tiny meatballs cook quickly, so it's perfect for a weeknight supper, especially on a cold fall or winter night.

1 pound 90/10 ground beef

1 medium yellow onion, peeled and grated

3 large eggs, divided

⅓ cup plus ½ cup Arborio rice, divided

1 teaspoon ground allspice

⅛ teaspoon ground nutmeg

¾ teaspoon salt, divided

¾ teaspoon ground black pepper, divided

8 cups low-sodium chicken broth

1 tablespoon all-purpose flour

2 tablespoons water

3 tablespoons lemon juice

SERVES 8

Per Serving:

Calories	218
Fat	8g
Sodium	342mg
Carbohydrates	18g
Fiber	1g
Sugar	1g
Protein	19g

1 In a large bowl, combine beef, onion, 1 egg, ⅓ cup rice, allspice, nutmeg, ¼ teaspoon salt, and ¼ teaspoon pepper. Roll mixture into 1" balls. Set aside.

2 Add broth, meatballs, remaining ½ cup rice, and remaining ½ teaspoon each salt and pepper to an Instant Pot®. Close lid, press the Manual or Pressure Cook button, and adjust time to 5 minutes. When the timer beeps, let pressure release naturally for 10 minutes. Quick-release any remaining pressure until the float valve drops. Press the Cancel button and open lid.

3 In a large bowl, whisk together flour and water to form a slurry. Whisk in lemon juice and remaining 2 eggs. Continuing to whisk vigorously, slowly add a ladle of soup liquid into egg mixture. Continue whisking and slowly add another 3–4 ladles of soup (one at a time) into egg mixture.

4 Slowly stir egg mixture back into the soup.

5 Allow soup to cool for 5 minutes, then serve it immediately.

Spanish Beef Stew

SERVES 8

Per Serving:

Calories	329
Fat	11g
Sodium	478mg
Carbohydrates	38g
Fiber	4g
Sugar	4g
Protein	18g

For extra flavor, use wrinkled Turkish olives (or other Mediterranean olives) instead of the standard stuffed olives found in the grocery store.

1 tablespoon olive oil

2 cloves garlic, peeled and sliced

1 medium yellow onion, peeled and sliced

3 slices bacon, cut into 1" pieces

1 pound stew beef, cubed

3 large Roma tomatoes, diced

1 bay leaf, crumbled

¼ teaspoon dried sage

¼ teaspoon dried marjoram

½ teaspoon paprika

½ teaspoon ground cumin

1 teaspoon salt

2 tablespoons vinegar

1 cup beef stock

½ cup white wine

4 medium russet potatoes, peeled and sliced

⅓ cup pitted, sliced green olives

2 tablespoons chopped fresh parsley

1 Press the Sauté button on an Instant Pot® and heat oil. Sauté garlic, onion, bacon, and beef until bacon and beef are cooked through and onion is soft, 7–8 minutes. Press the Cancel button.

2 Add tomatoes, bay leaf, sage, marjoram, paprika, cumin, salt, vinegar, stock, and wine. Close lid, press the Slow Cooker button, and adjust time to 5 hours.

3 Press the Cancel button and open lid. Add potatoes, olives, and parsley. Close lid, press the Slow Cooker button, and adjust time to 1 hour.

4 Serve immediately.

Beef Stew with Carrots

Pressure cookers are great for breaking down tougher cuts of meat in a short period of time. They are safe and a must-have appliance in your kitchen.

SERVES 6

Per Serving:

Calories	505
Fat	33g
Sodium	527mg
Carbohydrates	12g
Fiber	3g
Sugar	5g
Protein	32g

2 pounds stewing beef, cut into large pieces

⅓ cup olive oil

1 cup canned diced tomatoes

1 cup dry white wine

3 cloves garlic, peeled and smashed

1 large yellow onion, peeled and roughly chopped

3 bay leaves

3 sprigs fresh thyme

1 teaspoon dried rosemary

6 medium carrots, peeled and thinly sliced

5 whole peppercorns

4 whole cloves

1 teaspoon sea salt, divided

1 teaspoon ground black pepper, divided

1 tablespoon cornstarch

1 tablespoon cold water

1 Place beef, oil, tomatoes, wine, garlic, onion, bay leaves, thyme, rosemary, carrots, peppercorns, cloves, ½ teaspoon salt, and ½ teaspoon pepper in a pressure cooker and stir well. Add enough water to cover by 1".

2 Lock the lid into place. Bring to high pressure over medium heat; maintain for 45 minutes. Remove from heat and quick-release the pressure.

3 Uncover and place pan over medium heat. Remove and discard bay leaves and thyme sprigs. Stir stew and season with remaining ½ teaspoon each salt and pepper.

4 In a small bowl, stir together cornstarch with water. Add mixture to the pan and cook, stirring, for 2–3 minutes until thickened.

5 Serve hot.

Veal Osso Buco

SERVES 6

Per Serving:

Calories	445
Fat	13g
Sodium	1,328mg
Carbohydrates	21g
Fiber	2g
Sugar	3g
Protein	50g

SLOW COOKED TASTE

Osso buco is a cut of beef from the shank of a calf. If there's a dish that exemplifies "slow cooking," it's osso buco, but the pressure cooker makes quick work of this robust dish. If you plan ahead, you can make it the day before you plan to serve it and reheat it before serving. It's one of those dishes that only improves with time.

Osso buco is a Northern Italian dish made with veal shanks. It's easy enough for even novice cooks, and it makes a great go-to meal for entertaining family or friends.

¾ cup all-purpose flour

6 (1-pound) veal shanks, tied into rounds

2 teaspoons sea salt

½ teaspoon ground black pepper

3 tablespoons olive oil

1 medium yellow onion, peeled and diced

1 stalk celery, trimmed and diced

2 large carrots, peeled and diced

1 medium lemon, zest peeled off into strips

4 cloves garlic, peeled and smashed

¾ cup chopped fresh parsley, divided

3 bay leaves

2 tablespoons tomato paste

1½ cups red wine

2½ cups veal, beef, or chicken stock

1 tablespoon plus 1 teaspoon fresh thyme leaves, divided

2 tablespoons grated lemon zest

1 tablespoon minced garlic

1. Place flour in a shallow bowl. Season shanks with salt and pepper, then dredge in flour.
2. Heat oil in a pressure cooker over medium heat. In batches, cook shanks until browned on both sides, 6–7 minutes per side. Transfer to a plate and set aside.
3. To the pressure cooker, add onion, celery, carrots, lemon peel, smashed garlic, ¼ cup parsley, and bay leaves. Sauté over medium heat for 8 minutes. Stir in tomato paste and cook for 2 minutes.
4. Add wine, stock, and 1 tablespoon thyme and bring to a boil. Add shanks and any juices that have collected. Lock lid into place.
5. Bring to high pressure; maintain for 20 minutes. Remove from heat and allow pressure to release naturally for 15 minutes, then quick-release the remaining pressure. Uncover; remove and discard bay leaves.
6. Make the gremolata: In a small bowl, stir together remaining ½ cup parsley, lemon zest, minced garlic, and remaining 1 teaspoon thyme. Serve veal topped with gremolata.

CHAPTER 7

Baking Dish and Casserole Dishes

Gemista (Baked Stuffed Vegetables)

SERVES 6

Per Serving:

Calories	450
Fat	15g
Sodium	997mg
Carbohydrates	71g
Fiber	6g
Sugar	9g
Protein	9g

Stuffed vegetables are made regularly in the summer months in Greece. Of course, you can make this in the cooler months, but this dish shines with ripe, locally grown vegetables.

6 medium tomatoes, tops and insides removed and reserved

6 medium bell peppers, tops and insides removed, tops reserved

¼ cup plus 2 tablespoons extra-virgin olive oil, divided

12 scallions, trimmed and thinly sliced

4 cloves garlic, peeled and minced

2 cups long-grain white rice

1 cup chopped fresh dill

1 cup chopped fresh parsley

¼ cup chopped fresh mint

½ teaspoon ground black pepper

2½ teaspoons salt, divided

1 Preheat oven to 400°F.

2 Place hollowed-out tomatoes and bell peppers in a 13" × 9" baking dish. The vegetables should fit tightly so they don't topple over. Use a smaller baking dish if necessary.

3 Place tomato pulp in a food processor or blender and pulse to purée. Transfer to a medium bowl. Add ¼ cup oil, scallions, garlic, rice, dill, parsley, mint, black pepper, and 2 teaspoons salt and stir to combine.

4 Use a spoon to stuff each vegetable with rice mixture, pushing the filling down with your fingers if necessary. Cover with the reserved tops.

5 Drizzle with remaining 2 tablespoons oil and sprinkle with remaining ½ teaspoon salt. Bake uncovered for 60–70 minutes until vegetables are golden brown on top.

6 Serve warm or at room temperature.

Stuffed Long Peppers

This dish is made throughout Greece and much of the Mediterranean. You can also use tomatoes, zucchini, or eggplant. If you can hollow out a vegetable, it can be stuffed with the rice and herb mixture.

6 medium Cubanelle peppers

6 medium Red Shepherd peppers

2 cups finely diced yellow onion

4 cloves garlic, peeled and minced

1 cup extra-virgin olive oil, divided

1 cup tomato purée or tomato sauce

2 cups Arborio rice

1 cup chopped fresh parsley

½ cup chopped fresh dill

¼ cup chopped fresh mint

1½ teaspoons sea salt, divided

1 teaspoon ground black pepper, divided

SERVES 6	
Per Serving:	
Calories	490
Fat	37g
Sodium	388mg
Carbohydrates	36g
Fiber	9g
Sugar	18g
Protein	5g

1 Preheat oven to 375°F.

2 Use a small, sharp knife to carefully slice almost all the way through the tops of peppers, leaving the tops hinged. Use a small spoon to scoop out seeds and ribs. Set aside.

3 Add onion, garlic, ½ cup oil, tomato purée, rice, parsley, dill, mint, ½ teaspoon salt, and ½ teaspoon black pepper to a large bowl. Stir to combine.

4 Use the small spoon to stuff peppers with rice mixture and cover with tops. Lay stuffed peppers on their sides in a large baking dish. Pour remaining ½ cup oil over peppers.

5 Add enough hot water to the pan so the level of liquid comes up a quarter of the way around the peppers. Sprinkle with remaining 1 teaspoon salt and ½ teaspoon black pepper.

6 Bake uncovered for 70–90 minutes until peppers are golden brown on top and rice is cooked through. Serve hot.

Spinach and Feta Gratin

SERVES 6

Per Serving:

Calories	298
Fat	21g
Sodium	323mg
Carbohydrates	14g
Fiber	3g
Sugar	5g
Protein	16g

IF IT'S NOT GREEK, IT'S NOT REAL FETA...

Greek feta cheese has a lower overall fat content and is more nutritionally beneficial than most other commercially available cheeses, including imitation cow's milk "feta" cheeses being produced and sold in North America and elsewhere.

A gratin like this is so versatile. It's great warm or cold, it's good for brunch or a light dinner, and it can even be used as a make-ahead breakfast. Cut the gratin into six pieces, wrap each piece separately, and keep them in the refrigerator for up to 5 days or in the freezer for up to 3 weeks.

4 bunches (about 2½ pounds) spinach, trimmed and roughly chopped

3 bunches scallions, trimmed and chopped

¼ cup extra-virgin olive oil

¼ cup all-purpose flour

2 cups whole milk

4 large eggs, beaten

½ cup chopped fresh dill

½ cup grated graviera or Gruyère cheese

½ teaspoon ground nutmeg

½ cup crumbled feta cheese

1 Preheat oven to 375°F.
2 Place spinach, scallions, oil, flour, and milk in a large bowl and toss to coat. Add eggs, dill, graviera, and nutmeg and stir well.
3 Transfer mixture to a medium deep baking dish and spread evenly. Top with feta.
4 Bake for 45–50 minutes until just golden brown on top. Serve warm or at room temperature.

Frittata

FOR THE MEAT LOVER

If you think a breakfast just isn't breakfast without pork, consider adding chopped bacon, sausage, or ham to this frittata.

This Italian egg dish is like a quiche without a crust. It's a great way to use leftover potatoes and any vegetables in your refrigerator. Frittata is both a terrific breakfast dish and an easy weeknight supper.

2 medium yellow bell peppers, seeded and sliced

2 medium red bell peppers, seeded and sliced

2 medium green bell peppers, seeded and sliced

1 large red onion, peeled and sliced

1 teaspoon salt, divided

½ teaspoon ground black pepper, divided

2 teaspoons extra-virgin olive oil

1 (32-ounce) package refrigerated precooked potato wedges

3 large eggs

6 large egg whites

1 cup plain low-fat Greek yogurt

1 cup whole milk

3 ounces Fontina or Gouda cheese, grated

1 tablespoon chopped fresh oregano leaves

1 Preheat oven to 375°F.

2 Place bell peppers, onion, ½ teaspoon salt, and ¼ teaspoon black pepper in a medium baking dish. Drizzle with oil and toss to coat. Transfer to a large baking dish. Bake for 10 minutes.

3 Remove baking dish from oven and add potatoes. Stir gently to mix.

4 In a medium bowl, whisk together eggs, egg whites, yogurt, milk, cheese, and remaining ½ teaspoon salt and ¼ teaspoon black pepper. Pour egg mixture into baking dish over vegetables.

5 Bake until eggs are completely set, approximately 30 minutes. Sprinkle with oregano and serve.

Greek Roasted Potatoes

Lemony roasted potatoes are a must for any Greek feast and are often paired with roast lamb, beef, or chicken.

8 large Yukon Gold or russet potatoes, peeled and sliced lengthwise into wedges

½ cup extra-virgin olive oil

2 tablespoons fresh lemon juice

½ teaspoon ground black pepper

1 teaspoon salt

1 teaspoon dried oregano

½ cup hot water

SERVES 12	
Per Serving:	
Calories	275
Fat	9g
Sodium	206mg
Carbohydrates	45g
Fiber	3g
Sugar	2g
Protein	5g

1 Preheat oven to 425°F.

2 In a large bowl, combine potatoes, oil, lemon juice, pepper, salt, oregano, and water. Stir to coat.

3 Empty the bowl into a large, deep baking dish. Bake for 20 minutes. Stir potatoes and bake for another 20 minutes or until fork-tender.

Roasted Potatoes with Vegetables

SERVES 6

Per Serving:

Calories	160
Fat	5g
Sodium	236mg
Carbohydrates	28g
Fiber	4g
Sugar	4g
Protein	3g

This dish serves double duty as a treat for breakfast or as a side dish at dinner.

2 tablespoons olive oil

3 medium baking potatoes, peeled and chopped

1 medium sweet potato, peeled and chopped

3 large carrots, peeled and chopped

1 medium yellow onion, peeled and chopped

½ pound button mushrooms

½ teaspoon salt

1 teaspoon ground black pepper

1 Preheat oven to 400°F.

2 Combine all ingredients in a large baking dish and stir to mix. Roast until tender, about 30–45 minutes. Serve warm or at room temperature.

Briam (Greek Roasted Vegetables)

Briam is one of the original one pot meals. All you need to do is cut up some vegetables and layer the ingredients in a roasting pan. It's a great summer dish for when no one wants to be in the kitchen all day.

4 tablespoons extra-virgin olive oil, divided

3 medium russet potatoes, peeled and sliced

1 large eggplant, trimmed and sliced

3 medium zucchini, trimmed and sliced

6 cloves garlic, peeled and sliced

1 large carrot, peeled and sliced

2 medium yellow onions, peeled and thinly sliced, divided

1 cup chopped fresh parsley, divided

1 teaspoon salt, divided

¾ teaspoon ground black pepper, divided

2 medium tomatoes, sliced

1 large red bell pepper, seeded and sliced

1 medium Cubanelle pepper, seeded and sliced

½ cup tomato purée

4 scallions, trimmed and chopped

3 bay leaves

2 teaspoons dried oregano

3 cups water

SERVES 6	
Per Serving:	
Calories	230
Fat	10g
Sodium	458mg
Carbohydrates	34g
Fiber	7g
Sugar	8g
Protein	5g

1 Preheat oven to 425°F. Brush a large baking dish with 2 tablespoons oil.

2 Layer potato slices on the bottom of prepared pan, followed by a layer of eggplant slices and a layer of zucchini slices. Top with garlic, carrot, and half the onion slices. Sprinkle with ½ cup parsley and ½ teaspoon each salt and black pepper.

3 Add a layer of tomato slices, bell pepper, Cubanelle pepper, and remaining onion slices. Top with tomato purée, scallions, bay leaves, and oregano. Carefully pour water over vegetables.

4 Drizzle with remaining 2 tablespoons oil and season with remaining ½ teaspoon salt and ¼ teaspoon black pepper.

5 Bake for 1 hour until the top is golden brown and the liquid has thickened. Remove and discard bay leaves. Sprinkle with remaining ½ cup parsley before serving.

Cheesy Baked Penne

This recipe is so easy to prepare: Gather your ingredients, place them in a baking dish, and bake until bubbling and a little brown on top. The mozzarella is key here, as it gets gooey and melts inside the penne. You can switch up the other cheeses to your liking.

4 cups cooked penne

1 (24-ounce) jar marinara sauce

2 cups heavy cream

1 cup shredded mozzarella cheese

½ cup shredded Gouda cheese

8 tablespoons grated Parmesan cheese, divided

¼ cup whole-milk ricotta cheese

¼ cup crumbled blue cheese

½ cup fresh basil leaves

1 teaspoon sea salt

½ teaspoon ground black pepper

⅛ teaspoon crushed red pepper flakes

¼ cup extra-virgin olive oil

2 tablespoons thinly sliced basil

SERVES 8

Per Serving:

Calories	506
Fat	39g
Sodium	1,032mg
Carbohydrates	25g
Fiber	2g
Sugar	7g
Protein	15g

1 Preheat oven to 500°F.
2 Place penne, marinara sauce, cream, mozzarella, Gouda, 6 table-spoons Parmesan, ricotta, blue cheese, whole basil leaves, salt, black pepper, and pepper flakes in a large bowl. Toss until combined.
3 Transfer mixture to a large, deep baking dish and spread evenly. Drizzle with oil.
4 Bake for 15–20 minutes until casserole bubbles around the edges and is slightly brown on top.
5 Allow to rest for 5 minutes. Serve topped with sliced basil and the remaining 2 tablespoons Parmesan.

Artichoke Moussaka

SERVES 8

Per Serving:

Calories	485
Fat	23g
Sodium	1,082mg
Carbohydrates	49g
Fiber	7g
Sugar	11g
Protein	22g

IS IT GREEK OR IS IT TURKISH?

Moussaka is claimed by both Greek and Turkish cuisines. A version of the meat and eggplant casserole has been made by Turkish cooks since the 13th century. It was given the name "moussaka" in the mid 1800s. After the reign of the Ottoman Empire, the Greeks "reinvented" the dish by adding a white sauce on top. Both versions are delicious!

This recipe is a refreshing take on classic moussaka, which is usually made with eggplant.

1 cup coarse bread crumbs, divided

2 large russet potatoes, peeled and thinly sliced with a mandoline

½ cup plain whole-milk Greek yogurt

¼ cup all-purpose flour

4 cups whole milk

4 large eggs

1 cup grated kefalotyri or Romano cheese, divided

1½ teaspoons sea salt, divided

¾ teaspoon ground black pepper, divided

2 cups fresh green peas or thawed frozen peas

2 bunches scallions, trimmed and sliced

10 frozen artichoke hearts, thawed and sliced

1½ tablespoons lemon juice

1 cup crumbled feta cheese, divided

¼ cup chopped fresh dill, divided

2 tablespoons chopped fresh oregano, divided

¼ cup extra-virgin olive oil

1 Preheat oven to 375°F. Grease a 13" × 9" baking dish.

2 Sprinkle ¼ cup bread crumbs on the bottom of the baking dish and press some into the sides. Cover with potato slices in slightly overlapping rows.

3 In a medium bowl, combine yogurt, flour, milk, eggs, ½ cup kefalotyri, ½ teaspoon salt, and ¼ teaspoon pepper. Whisk until smooth. In a separate medium bowl, combine peas and scallions. Place artichoke hearts in a small bowl and toss with lemon juice.

4 Ladle half the sauce over potatoes, then spoon half the pea mixture over sauce. Top with ¼ cup bread crumbs, ½ cup feta, 2 tablespoons dill, and 1 tablespoon oregano. Add a layer of artichokes and ¼ cup bread crumbs. Top with remaining pea mixture, then ½ cup feta, 2 tablespoons dill, and 1 tablespoon oregano. Cover with remaining ¼ cup bread crumbs.

5 Pour remaining sauce over the layers, drizzle with oil, and top with remaining ½ cup kefalotyri. Sprinkle with remaining 1 teaspoon salt and ½ teaspoon pepper. Bake for 50–55 minutes until the top is golden brown. Allow to rest for at least 30 minutes before serving.

Ruffled Phyllo Cheese Pie

This shortcut cheese pie uses store-bought phyllo. Buy phyllo from a store that sells a lot of it, so you can be sure your package is fresh and therefore easy to work with.

1 tablespoon olive oil

½ cup plain whole milk Greek yogurt

3 large eggs

2 cups crumbled feta cheese

2 cups whole-milk ricotta cheese

¾ teaspoon ground black pepper

1 (16-ounce) package phyllo dough, thawed

½ cup unsalted butter, melted

1 (12-ounce) can club soda or sparkling water

SERVES 8

Per Serving:

Calories	581
Fat	36g
Sodium	899mg
Carbohydrates	43g
Fiber	2g
Sugar	3g
Protein	20g

1 Preheat oven to 375°F. Brush the bottom of a 16" × 12" deep baking dish with oil.

2 Place yogurt and eggs in a large bowl and beat with a hand mixer until smooth. Stir in feta, ricotta, and pepper. Set aside.

3 Place a sheet of phyllo on a flat work surface. Pour 3 tablespoons cheese mixture evenly over the phyllo sheet. Fold over the phyllo sheet 1" from the bottom. With your fingers holding the fold, continue to fold and pinch the phyllo together so it resembles accordion pleats. Place in prepared baking dish. Repeat with remaining phyllo and filling.

4 Brush phyllo with melted butter. Open the club soda and immediately pour it over phyllo.

5 Bake for 45–60 minutes until golden brown.

6 Allow to cool for 5 minutes. Cut into squares and serve.

WORKING WITH PHYLLO

If you are intimidated by handling phyllo pastry, this recipe is for you. It is a very forgiving recipe, so don't worry about the phyllo sticking a bit or tearing. Follow the instructions as close as you can and you will get a great looking and tasting pie.

Baked Elephant Beans with Peppers

Elephant beans are also known as "gigantes" or "giant lima beans." You can soak dried beans overnight, but the canned variety is a great shortcut ingredient.

SERVES 4

Per Serving:	
Calories	494
Fat	29g
Sodium	1,272mg
Carbohydrates	47g
Fiber	13g
Sugar	8g
Protein	15g

2 (19-ounce) cans elephant (gigantes) beans or lima beans, drained and rinsed

½ cup olive oil

2 medium leeks (white parts only), trimmed and sliced

1 medium carrot, peeled and grated

1 medium Red Shepherd pepper, stemmed and sliced into rings

1 medium Cubanelle pepper, stemmed and sliced into rings

1 small hot banana pepper, seeded, stemmed, and sliced

3 cloves garlic, peeled and minced

½ cup tomato purée

1 tablespoon tomato paste

1 teaspoon sugar

1 teaspoon smoked paprika

1½ teaspoons sea salt

¼ teaspoon ground black pepper

3 bay leaves

½ cup chopped fresh parsley

1 Preheat oven to 375°F.
2 Place beans, oil, leeks, carrot, peppers, garlic, tomato purée, tomato paste, sugar, paprika, salt, black pepper, and bay leaves in a large bowl and toss to combine. Transfer mixture to a large baking dish.
3 Add enough hot water to just cover ingredients. Bake for 45 minutes or until most of the liquid has been absorbed.
4 Remove and discard bay leaves. Garnish with parsley and serve.

Zucchini Parmesan

Use plain or seasoned bread crumbs for this recipe. Also, try adding thin-sliced fresh basil or chopped oregano for flair and extra flavor.

2 large egg whites

1 cup skim milk

½ cup dried bread crumbs

3 medium zucchini, trimmed and cut into ½" slices

2 cups marinara sauce

6 ounces part-skim shredded mozzarella cheese

1 Preheat oven to 375°F.

2 Beat egg whites and milk in a shallow dish. Place bread crumbs in another shallow dish. Dip zucchini into egg mixture, then into bread crumbs. Set aside.

3 Ladle enough sauce into a large casserole or baking dish to cover the bottom. Cover the sauce with a single layer of breaded zucchini. Top with half of the cheese, then the remaining sauce. Layer the remaining zucchini over the sauce, followed by the remaining cheese. Bake for 15–20 minutes until cheese melts and begins to brown.

SERVES 6

Per Serving:

Calories	199
Fat	8g
Sodium	682mg
Carbohydrates	20g
Fiber	3g
Sugar	10g
Protein	13g

PARMESAN

Parmesan is best known as a type of cheese, but the term "Parmesan" also loosely refers to a type of cooking—for example, Chicken Parmesan. Any type of Parmesan dish indicates the presence of some type of cheese, but not necessarily Parmesan cheese.

Pasta Shells Stuffed with Roasted Red Peppers and Feta

Per Serving:

Calories	460
Fat	25g
Sodium	1,143mg
Carbohydrates	40g
Fiber	5g
Sugar	13g
Protein	18g

ROASTED PEPPERS

A jar of roasted red peppers is a versatile convenience product. Keep several on hand. They can be served as part of an antipasto platter, made into a sauce, or in this case, part of a filling for pasta.

This vegetarian dish is loaded with flavor from the roasted peppers and the briny feta. Look for the largest pasta shells—they're easier to stuff with the filling.

7 ounces whole-milk ricotta cheese

7 ounces feta cheese, crumbled

5 roasted red bell peppers, peeled, seeded, and chopped

⅓ cup fresh basil leaves

1 tablespoon extra-virgin olive oil

½ teaspoon salt

¼ teaspoon ground black pepper

1 (24-ounce) jar marinara sauce

18 cooked jumbo pasta shells

½ cup heavy cream

½ cup grated Parmesan cheese

1 Preheat oven to 350°F.

2 Place ricotta, feta, roasted peppers, basil, oil, salt, and black pepper in a food processor or blender. Process until smooth.

3 Spread marinara sauce on the bottom of a large, round baking dish.

4 Use a small spoon to fill pasta shells with the ricotta mixture. Place filled shells in prepared baking dish in a circular pattern. Dot each shell with cream and top with Parmesan.

5 Bake for 30 minutes. Allow to cool for 5 minutes before serving.

Baked Feta

SERVES 6

Per Serving:

Calories	147
Fat	13g
Sodium	349mg
Carbohydrates	3g
Fiber	1g
Sugar	2g
Protein	6g

LITTLE DIPPERS

Slice a baguette into 1/8"-thick slices. Brush lightly with olive oil and sprinkle with dried tarragon and rosemary. Bake at 350°F for 10 minutes or until crisp.

Roma tomatoes are perfect for this appetizer because they have less water and fewer seeds, and are usually sweeter than other tomato varieties. Don't forget to serve lots of crusty bread with this dish to sop up all the tasty juices.

1 (8-ounce) slab feta cheese

2 tablespoons extra-virgin olive oil, divided

1 large Roma tomato, thinly sliced

1 large banana or sweet pepper, seeded and thinly sliced

1/4 teaspoon crushed red pepper flakes

1/4 teaspoon dried oregano

1 Preheat oven to 400°F.

2 Place cheese and 1 tablespoon oil in a small baking dish. Top with alternating layers of tomato and pepper slices. Drizzle remaining 1 tablespoon oil and sprinkle pepper flakes and oregano over tomato and pepper slices.

3 Cover baking dish tightly with foil and bake for 20 minutes. Serve immediately.

Bouyiourdi

This dish is a hot, cheesy Greek fondue that's perfect with crusty bread.

1 large tomato, diced, divided

½ cup crumbled feta cheese

½ cup grated kasseri or Gouda cheese, divided

1 small banana pepper, seeded and sliced

1 tablespoon extra-virgin olive oil

¼ teaspoon crushed red pepper flakes

½ teaspoon oregano

1 Preheat oven to 400°F.

2 Place half of the tomato on the bottom of a ramekin or small baking dish. Top with feta and ¼ cup kasseri. Top cheeses with banana peppers, remaining tomatoes, and remaining ¼ cup kasseri. Drizzle with oil, then sprinkle with pepper flakes and oregano.

3 Cover dish tightly with foil and bake for 20 minutes or until cheese is bubbling. Serve immediately.

SERVES 6

Per Serving:

Calories	93
Fat	7g
Sodium	191mg
Carbohydrates	2g
Fiber	1g
Sugar	2g
Protein	4g

FRESH OR CANNED?

This dish is best made when tomatoes are in season, sweet and full of flavor. But you can make it any time using canned diced tomatoes. Strain the tomatoes first and assemble as per instructions. Next time you're out grocery shopping, buy a can or two of diced tomatoes for your pantry.

Baked Fish "Plaki"

The word plaki *refers to a dish that is baked in the oven with potatoes and vegetables. For a more dramatic presentation, use 1 (2-pound) fish.*

2 (1-pound) whole red snapper, trout, or grouper, scaled and gutted

1 teaspoon salt

¾ teaspoon ground black pepper

1 large tomato, diced

1½ cups chopped fresh parsley, divided

5 cloves garlic, peeled and roughly chopped, divided

4 tablespoons chopped fresh oregano, divided

4 medium russet potatoes, peeled and cut into wedges

2 medium Cubanelle peppers, stemmed and sliced into rings

1 large tomato, halved and cut into slices

½ cup extra-virgin olive oil

3 tablespoons all-purpose flour

1 teaspoon sweet paprika

1 cup water

SERVES 4	
Per Serving:	
Calories	578
Fat	29g
Sodium	656mg
Carbohydrates	54g
Fiber	7g
Sugar	6g
Protein	27g

1 Preheat oven to 350°F.

2 Season fish (inside and out) with salt and pepper. In a small bowl, combine diced tomato, ½ cup parsley, 2 cloves garlic, and 2 table-spoons oregano. Stuff mixture into the fish cavities.

3 Spread remaining 1 cup parsley in an even layer in the bottom of a large baking dish. Top with layers of potatoes, Cubanelle peppers, and sliced tomato. Sprinkle with the remaining 3 cloves garlic and 2 tablespoons oregano. Place fish on top of mixture.

4 In a large measuring cup, add oil, flour, and paprika and whisk together to incorporate. Pour flour mixture over fish.

5 Pour water around edges of the casserole. Bake for 40–45 minutes until fish flakes easily and potatoes are fork-tender.

6 Serve immediately.

Roast Cod with Tomato-Caper Crust

SERVES 4

Per Serving:

Calories	461
Fat	23g
Sodium	908mg
Carbohydrates	31g
Fiber	5g
Sugar	8g
Protein	28g

Capers grow wild in the Mediterranean region. They're sold in jars, preserved in a brine. Give them a light rinse and add them to fish or salad dishes for a wonderful umami lift.

4 (5-ounce) cod fillets

1 teaspoon sea salt

½ teaspoon ground black pepper

4 large ripe plum tomatoes, diced

⅓ cup fresh parsley leaves

2 teaspoons dried Greek oregano

3 cloves garlic, peeled

2 tablespoons drained and rinsed capers

½ cup dry white wine

¼ cup plus 2 tablespoons extra-virgin olive oil, divided

1 bunch scallions, trimmed and thinly sliced

1 cup fresh bread crumbs

1 Season fillets with salt and pepper and set aside for 30 minutes.
2 Place tomatoes, parsley, oregano, garlic, capers, and wine in a food processor and pulse until mixture is blended but not smooth. Set aside for 30 minutes.
3 Preheat oven to 400°F.
4 Pour ¼ cup oil on the bottom of a 13" × 9" baking dish. Sprinkle scallions over oil. Place cod on top of scallions. Spoon tomato mixture over fish and sprinkle with bread crumbs. Drizzle with remaining 2 tablespoons oil.
5 Bake for 25–30 minutes until bread crumb topping forms a crisp, light brown crust.
6 Allow to cool for 5 minutes before serving.

Aegean Baked Sole

Turbot, halibut, or flounder can be substituted for the sole in this recipe.

2 medium lemons, divided

8 (6-ounce) sole fillets

½ teaspoon salt

½ teaspoon ground black pepper

4 tablespoons extra-virgin olive oil, divided

1 teaspoon dried oregano

¼ cup capers

4 tablespoons chopped fresh dill

2 tablespoons chopped scallions

1 Preheat oven to 350°F.

2 Slice one lemon into thin slices, then cut slices in half. Set aside. Season fillets with salt and pepper.

3 Pour 2 tablespoons oil into a medium baking dish. Layer fish and lemon slices alternately.

4 Sprinkle oregano, capers, dill, and scallions over fish and lemon slices. Drizzle remaining 2 tablespoons oil and squeeze juice of remaining lemon over dish.

5 Cover and bake for 30 minutes. Serve immediately.

SERVES 8

Per Serving:

Calories	167
Fat	10g
Sodium	676mg
Carbohydrates	2g
Fiber	0g
Sugar	0g
Protein	18g

LEMON LIFT

In the Mediterranean, lemon is paired often with fish and seafood, and it gives dishes a nice citrus pop. When serving the dish, don't be shy about drizzling it with more olive oil and adding another squeeze of lemon.

Roasted Branzino with Potatoes and Fennel

FRESHNESS COUNTS

Whole fish may involve a little bit more work to eat, when you have to work around the bones, but if you live near the water, it's worth it to find a shop that sells fresh, whole fish. A fresh fish will always smell of the sea. Settle for nothing else.

This easy meal contains all the flavors of the Mediterranean seaside, and it makes a great special occasion splurge meal. Branzino is sometimes called "European sea bass" in fish markets. Serve with a side of sautéed garlicky greens.

2 small (1-pound) whole branzino or black sea bass

2 tablespoons extra-virgin olive oil, divided

½ teaspoon salt, divided

½ teaspoon ground black pepper, divided

¼ cup fennel fronds, divided

4 small red potatoes, peeled and halved

1 small yellow onion, peeled and sliced

1 cup thinly sliced fennel

1½ tablespoons lemon juice

2 teaspoons grated lemon zest

2 tablespoons chopped fresh parsley

¼ cup dry white wine

½ cup vegetable stock

2 large tomatoes, sliced

4 scallions, trimmed and chopped

4 pitted Kalamata olives

2 teaspoons drained and rinsed capers

½ medium lemon, cut into wedges

1 Preheat oven to 450°F. Spray a large, deep baking dish with non-stick cooking spray.

2 Brush fish with 1 tablespoon oil. Season inside and out with ¼ teaspoon each salt and pepper. Stuff half of the fennel fronds into the cavities of the fish and set aside.

3 In prepared baking dish, place potatoes, onion, sliced fennel, remaining 1 tablespoon oil, lemon juice, lemon zest, parsley, wine, and stock. Toss to mix and sprinkle with remaining ¼ teaspoon each salt and pepper. Layer tomato slices over potato mixture. Bake for 25 minutes.

4 Remove potato mixture from oven and top with fish. Sprinkle with scallions, olives, and capers. Bake for another 20–25 minutes until potatoes are fork-tender and fish is golden brown.

5 Top with remaining fennel fronds before serving with lemon wedges.

Baked Whiting with Potato Gratin

Whiting are smaller cousins of cod. They're light in flavor, affordable, and have few pin bones. This recipe may make a convert out of those squeamish about eating whole fish.

4 large Yukon Gold potatoes, cut into ¼" slices

2 medium yellow onions, peeled and sliced

1 cup sliced fennel

3 cloves garlic, peeled and smashed

2 teaspoons fresh thyme leaves

2 tablespoons chopped fresh parsley

5 tablespoons extra-virgin olive oil, divided

1 teaspoon sea salt, divided

1 teaspoon ground black pepper, divided

¼ cup dry white wine

½ cup vegetable or chicken stock

2 large ripe tomatoes, sliced

4 (¾-pound) whole whiting or hake, scaled and gutted

1 pound fresh clams, scrubbed

2 tablespoons chopped fresh fennel fronds

½ medium lemon, cut into wedges

SERVES 4	
Per Serving:	
Calories	537
Fat	20g
Sodium	1,094mg
Carbohydrates	47g
Fiber	8g
Sugar	8g
Protein	41g

1 Preheat oven to 450°F.

2 Place potatoes, onions, sliced fennel, garlic, thyme, parsley, 2 tablespoons oil, ½ teaspoon salt, and ½ teaspoon pepper in a large bowl. Toss to coat and transfer to a large baking dish. Add wine and stock and top with tomatoes.

3 Bake for 40 minutes or until potatoes are golden and fork-tender.

4 Remove from oven and switch to the broiler setting. Position a rack 6" below broiler.

5 Place fish on top of potato mixture and drizzle with 1 tablespoon oil. Season with remaining ½ teaspoon each salt and pepper. Scatter clams around fish. Broil for 8–10 minutes until fish is golden and crisp and clams open up.

6 Divide fish, clams, and potato mixture among four plates. Drizzle with remaining 2 tablespoons oil, sprinkle with fennel fronds, and serve with lemon wedges.

Shrimp Giouvetsi

SHRIMP SHELLS

Don't throw out your shrimp shells! Store shells in the freezer and use them to create delicious seafood stock.

This baked orzo casserole studded with vegetables and shrimp is sure to be a family favorite. Despite the short cooking time for the shrimp, their juices leave lots of flavor in the orzo.

1½ cups diced yellow onion

4 cloves garlic, peeled and finely chopped

½ cup diced green bell pepper

½ cup diced red bell pepper

¼ cup grated carrot

2 tablespoons extra-virgin olive oil

2 tablespoons tomato paste

2 tablespoons chopped fresh parsley

2 bay leaves

¾ teaspoon salt

¼ teaspoon ground black pepper

1 cup orzo

4 cups vegetable stock

¼ cup dry white wine

⅛ teaspoon crushed red pepper flakes

1 teaspoon ground star anise

3 tablespoons chopped fresh dill, divided

2 pounds large shrimp, peeled and deveined

1 Preheat oven to 375°F.

2 Place onion, garlic, bell peppers, carrot, oil, tomato paste, parsley, bay leaves, salt, and black pepper in a 3-quart baking dish. Stir to combine. Add orzo, stock, wine, pepper flakes, and star anise and stir again.

3 Bake for 30–35 minutes until most of the liquid has been absorbed.

4 Remove from oven and stir in 2 tablespoons dill. Place shrimp on top and return dish to oven. Bake for 5 minutes or until shrimp are pink and curl into a *C* shape.

5 Remove and discard bay leaves. Sprinkle with remaining 1 tablespoon dill before serving.

Scallops Saganaki

SERVES 4

Per Serving:

Calories	398
Fat	28g
Sodium	664mg
Carbohydrates	19g
Fiber	1g
Sugar	2g
Protein	10g

SAGANAKI

Most people associate the word "saganaki" with the flaming cheese version but there are many different types of saganaki dishes. It gets its name from the traditional two-handled vessel.

If you want to tone down the heat in this dish, use just half of a chili pepper. Be sure to have plenty of crusty bread to soak up the sauce.

16 large scallops

½ teaspoon salt

½ teaspoon ground black pepper

½ cup extra-virgin olive oil

⅓ cup dry white wine

2 ounces ouzo

2 tablespoons fresh lemon juice

6 cloves garlic, peeled and thinly sliced

1 small red chili pepper, stemmed and thinly sliced

½ teaspoon sweet paprika

1 small leek, trimmed and cut into matchsticks

⅔ cup bread crumbs

2 tablespoons chopped fresh parsley

1 large lemon, cut into wedges

1. Preheat oven to 450°F.
2. Season both sides of scallops with salt and black pepper. Place scallops in a medium baking dish. Set aside.
3. In a medium bowl, whisk together oil, wine, ouzo, lemon juice, garlic, chili pepper, and paprika. Pour sauce over scallops. Top with leeks and then bread crumbs.
4. Bake scallops on a middle rack for 8–10 minutes.
5. Set oven to broil and bake for another 2–3 minutes or until bread crumbs are golden.
6. Let scallops cool for 5 minutes, then top with parsley. Serve scallops with lemon wedges.

Chicken with Okra

This is a traditional Greek dish that's simple to make. Using frozen okra saves on prep time, and you'll find no difference in taste between frozen and fresh.

1 (3-pound) chicken, cut into 8 pieces

1 teaspoon salt, divided

¾ teaspoon ground black pepper, divided

4 large, very ripe tomatoes

1 large yellow onion, peeled

2 pounds small fresh okra or 2 (16-ounce) packages frozen baby okra

5 cloves garlic, peeled and sliced

4 whole allspice berries

½ cup chopped fresh parsley

1 cup chicken stock

SERVES 4	
Per Serving:	
Calories	452
Fat	22g
Sodium	934mg
Carbohydrates	17g
Fiber	7g
Sugar	7g
Protein	48g

1 Preheat oven to 375°F.
2 Sprinkle chicken pieces with ½ teaspoon salt and ¼ teaspoon pepper and place in a large baking dish.
3 Using a box grater, grate tomatoes into a large bowl, then grate onion into the bowl.
4 Add okra, garlic, allspice berries, parsley, and remaining ½ teaspoon each salt and pepper. Stir in stock.
5 Transfer okra mixture to the baking dish, covering the chicken. Bake covered for 50 minutes, then uncover and bake for 15 minutes more.
6 Set aside to cool for 5 minutes before serving.

Roast Pork and Potatoes

SERVES 8

Per Serving:

Calories	480
Fat	28g
Sodium	825mg
Carbohydrates	35g
Fiber	5g
Sugar	3g
Protein	22g

Meat and potatoes roasted together create the ultimate comfort food. The meat in this version is pork shoulder, a cut that has a bit of fat, which equals more flavor. You can trim some of the fat to suit your taste.

8 medium Yukon Gold potatoes, peeled and quartered

6 cloves garlic, peeled and smashed

½ cup extra-virgin olive oil

½ cup chicken stock

2 tablespoons Dijon mustard

3 tablespoons lemon juice

10 sprigs fresh thyme

3 sprigs of fresh rosemary

2 pounds boneless pork shoulder, cut into large chunks

2 teaspoons coarse sea salt, divided

1 teaspoon ground black pepper, divided

2 teaspoons sweet paprika

1 teaspoon dried Greek oregano

2 teaspoons fresh thyme leaves

¼ cup diced bacon

1　Preheat oven to 400°F.

2　Place potatoes in a large baking dish. Add garlic, oil, stock, mustard, lemon juice, thyme sprigs, and rosemary sprigs and toss until coated.

3　Place pork in a large bowl and add 1 teaspoon salt, ½ teaspoon pepper, paprika, oregano, and thyme leaves. Mix well with your hands.

4　Place pork mixture on top of potatoes and sprinkle with bacon.

5　Bake for 30 minutes. Carefully remove from oven and flip pork pieces. Sprinkle with the remaining 1 teaspoon salt and ½ teaspoon pepper. Return to oven and bake for 20 minutes or until pork is browned and potatoes are fork-tender.

6　Remove from oven and set aside to rest for 15 minutes. Remove and discard thyme and rosemary sprigs before serving.

Roast Pork with Potatoes and Quinces

A ripe quince looks like a yellow pear, but it's very tart and rarely eaten raw. When it's cooked, the flesh becomes softer and sweeter, with a spicy, complex aroma. If you can't find quince, use a firm, tart apple.

1½ pounds lean boneless pork loin

4 medium quinces, peeled and cored

12 medium baking potatoes, peeled and chopped

⅓ cup olive oil

¼ cup orange juice

1½ tablespoons grated orange zest

1½ teaspoons salt, divided

1 teaspoon ground black pepper, divided

SERVES 8	
Per Serving:	
Calories	462
Fat	14g
Sodium	506mg
Carbohydrates	63g
Fiber	7g
Sugar	4g
Protein	24g

1 Place pork in freezer for 30 minutes. Remove from freezer and cut into thin slices. Place each slice between two pieces of plastic wrap and pound into thin cutlets. Set aside.

2 Chop 2 quinces into chunks equal in size to potatoes. Cut remaining 2 quinces into very thin slices.

3 Place potatoes and chopped quinces in a large baking dish. Drizzle with oil and orange juice and toss to coat. Sprinkle with orange zest, ½ teaspoon salt, and ½ teaspoon pepper.

4 Preheat oven to 450°F.

5 Place a pork cutlet on a flat surface and cover with a quince slice. Roll up tightly and secure with a toothpick. Place pork roll in roasting pan. Repeat with remaining pork and quince. Sprinkle with the remaining 1 teaspoon salt and ½ teaspoon pepper.

6 Bake for 30 minutes. Remove from oven and flip pork rolls. Reduce heat to 400°F and return pan to the oven. Bake for 15–20 minutes until potatoes are fork-tender.

7 Serve hot.

Baked Rigatoni with Sausage and Eggplant

SERVES 6

Per Serving:

Calories	674
Fat	40g
Sodium	1,901mg
Carbohydrates	43g
Fiber	7g
Sugar	11g
Protein	35g

Hollow pasta like rigatoni allows for sauce and cheese to stick to the ridges and get into the center of the pasta. Penne also works well with this dish.

¾ pound Italian sausage links

1 large (1½-pound) eggplant, trimmed and cut into 1" pieces

1 large yellow onion, peeled and chopped

3 cloves garlic, peeled and chopped

¼ cup olive oil

1 pound rigatoni, cooked

1 (24-ounce) jar marinara sauce

1 pound fresh mozzarella, shredded

1 cup loosely packed fresh basil leaves

1 teaspoon sea salt

½ teaspoon ground black pepper

1 cup grated Parmesan cheese

1 Preheat oven to 400°F.

2 Place sausage, eggplant, onion, and garlic in a large, deep baking dish. Drizzle with oil and toss to coat. Cover and bake for 20 minutes.

3 Remove from oven and uncover baking dish. Remove sausage and cut into bite-sized pieces. Return sausage to baking dish. Stir in pasta, marinara, mozzarella, basil, salt, and pepper.

4 Baked uncovered for 10–12 minutes until cheese melts and casserole is bubbly.

5 Top with Parmesan before serving.

Roast Lamb, Potatoes, and Halloumi in Parchment

Halloumi cheese is a briny, firm cheese that melts well while holding its shape. It's available in Greek or Middle Eastern markets and can often be found in large supermarkets. Look for Cypriot halloumi.

6 (14-ounce) lamb shanks

1 whole head garlic, peeled, separated into cloves, and cut into slivers

12 medium Yukon Gold potatoes, peeled and cut into 1½" chunks

1 pound halloumi cheese, cubed

½ cup olive oil

3 tablespoons lemon juice

2 tablespoons grated lemon zest

1 tablespoon sweet paprika

1½ teaspoons sea salt, divided

1 teaspoon ground black pepper, divided

¼ cup melted unsalted butter

2 tablespoons fresh thyme leaves

6 small sprigs fresh rosemary

1 Preheat oven to 350°F.

2 Place shanks on a flat surface. Cut small slits all over shanks. Insert a sliver of garlic into each slit.

3 Add remaining garlic to a large bowl. Add potatoes, cheese, oil, lemon juice, lemon zest, paprika, ½ teaspoon salt, and ½ teaspoon pepper. Toss to combine. Set aside.

4 Brush butter over shanks. Season with remaining 1 teaspoon salt and ½ teaspoon pepper.

5 Place a large sheet of parchment paper over a large baking dish, centering the piece over the two long sides. Position a second large sheet over the two short sides. Arrange shanks in the paper-lined pan and top with potato mixture. Sprinkle with thyme and place a rosemary sprig on each shank. Bring the four ends of the parchment to the middle and twist to close. Tie closed with butcher's twine.

6 Bake for 2½ hours. Remove from oven and snip the twine to open up the package. Return to oven and bake for 15–20 minutes until lamb is browned and the internal temperature reaches 160°.

7 Transfer to a serving platter and serve.

SERVES 12

Per Serving:

Calories	580
Fat	29g
Sodium	402mg
Carbohydrates	36g
Fiber	5g
Sugar	3g
Protein	43g

KLEFTIKO

Many lamb in parchment dishes are inspired by a classic called Kleftiko. During Ottoman rule of Greece, Greek nationalist outlaws called Klefts would build a fire in a hole made in the ground and when glowing embers were ready, lamb was buried and the meat was cooked slowly. With this method, the Turks couldn't smell roasting meat or find the rebels.

CHAPTER 8

Simple Desserts

Byzantine Fruit Medley

SERVES 8

Per Serving:

Calories	156
Fat	0g
Sodium	3mg
Carbohydrates	38g
Fiber	4g
Sugar	32g
Protein	1g

A NOTE ON INGREDIENTS

This dessert will benefit from using a high-quality honey. Taste the fruits before and during cooking. You can scale back on the honey if the fruits are at their peak and add more honey if they need a sweet nudge. Choose a fruity and light unoaked wine for this dessert.

Feel free to experiment with the fruits you use in this recipe. Try fresh figs, white grapes, and pears

½ **cup red wine**

½ **cup honey**

2 **medium apples, peeled, cored, and diced**

2 **medium pears, peeled, cored, and diced**

3 **medium mandarin or clementine oranges, peeled and sectioned**

1 **cup pomegranate seeds (from 1 medium pomegranate)**

1 In a small saucepan, bring wine and honey to a boil over high heat. Boil for 3–4 minutes to evaporate most of the alcohol. Cool for 20 minutes.

2 Combine apples, pears, oranges, and pomegranate seeds in a medium bowl.

3 Pour wine mixture over fruit and refrigerate for at least 1 hour. Stir fruit a few times to ensure sauce covers everything. Serve cold.

Fig Compote with Star Anise

Dried figs are sweet and jammy and mix well with warm spices. Serve this compote warm or cool with plain yogurt or vanilla ice cream. It's also good over oatmeal for breakfast.

4 ounces dried figs

1 cup Mavrodaphne wine, port wine, or other fortified red wine

2 tablespoons honey

6 whole cloves

1 (3") cinnamon stick

1 whole star anise

1 teaspoon vanilla extract

1 (3" × 1½") strip lemon peel

½ teaspoon crushed red pepper flakes

1 Place all ingredients in a medium saucepan over medium heat and bring just to a boil. Reduce heat to low, cover, and simmer for 1½ hours.

2 Remove and discard cinnamon stick, star anise, and lemon peel.

3 Serve warm or refrigerate in a covered container for up to 3 months.

SERVES 4

Per Serving:

Calories	200
Fat	0g
Sodium	9mg
Carbohydrates	35g
Fiber	3g
Sugar	27g
Protein	1g

NEED CALCIUM AND FIBER?

Fresh or dried, figs are an excellent source of calcium and fiber, as well as many other nutrients. They are also rich in antioxidants and polyphenols.

Stuffed Figs

SERVES 4

Per Serving:

Calories	309
Fat	18g
Sodium	5mg
Carbohydrates	37g
Fiber	6g
Sugar	27g
Protein	6g

Purchase Kalamata dried string figs if you can find them, as they are larger and sweeter than most other commercially available varieties.

12 dried figs

24 walnut halves

2 tablespoons thyme honey

2 tablespoons sesame seeds

1 Snip tough stalk ends off figs. Slice the side of each fig and open with your fingers.

2 Stuff 2 walnut halves inside each fig and fold closed.

3 Arrange figs on a large platter. Drizzle with honey and sprinkle with sesame seeds. Serve immediately.

Poached Pears

Poached Pears are a great make-ahead dessert. Make them in the fall when pears are in season and many varieties are available in the store.

1½ cups sugar

4 cups water

½ cup honey

1 teaspoon vanilla extract

1 (3") cinnamon stick

3 (3" × 1½") strips lemon peel

4 large Bosc or Anjou pears, halved and cored

2 cups plain low-fat Greek yogurt

½ cup granola

1 Set a large, shallow pot that will fit all pear halves in one layer over medium heat. Add sugar, water, honey, vanilla, cinnamon stick, and lemon peel. Simmer for 10 minutes.

2 Cut a piece of parchment paper to fit over the top of the pot. Tear or cut a small hole in the middle.

3 Carefully place pears in the pot. Cover with parchment. Reduce heat to low and simmer pears for 15–17 minutes until they can easily be pierced with a knife.

4 Use a slotted spoon to remove pears from liquid and set aside. Continue simmering the poaching liquid for another 15 minutes until thickened. Remove and discard cinnamon stick and lemon peel. Set aside to cool for at least 20 minutes.

5 To serve, spoon a dollop of yogurt onto each of eight small plates and top with a pear half. Drizzle with a spoonful of the thickened poaching liquid and top with granola before serving.

SERVES 8

Per Serving:

Calories	356
Fat	3g
Sodium	27mg
Carbohydrates	79g
Fiber	4g
Sugar	70g
Protein	4g

DON'T HAVE GREEK YOGURT?

You can transform regular yogurt into thicker Greek-style yogurt. Spoon plain yogurt into a sieve over a bowl and set it in the refrigerator overnight. Discard the liquid and transfer the strained yogurt to a covered container.

Stewed Cinnamon Apples with Dates

FIRM APPLES

The best apples for baking, stewing, or braising are firm-fleshed varieties. Firm apples are most crisp when eaten raw. While a softer apple may be more appealing as a snack to eat out of hand, firmer apples hold up to cooking or baking and don't turn mushy. Granny Smith apples are among the firmest apples, but if you like a sweeter apple, try a Pink Lady instead.

Dates are naturally sweet, so you don't need to add any sugar to these apples. You can serve this dish hot, or let it cool and serve it over cold Greek yogurt.

4 large Granny Smith or Pink Lady apples, peeled, cored, and sliced

½ cup water

¼ cup chopped pitted dates

1 teaspoon ground cinnamon

¼ teaspoon vanilla extract

1 teaspoon unsalted butter

1 Place apples, water, dates, and cinnamon in an Instant Pot®. Close lid, press the Manual or Pressure Cook button, and adjust time to 3 minutes.

2 When the timer beeps, quick-release the pressure until the float valve drops. Press the Cancel button and open lid. Stir in vanilla and butter. Serve hot or chilled.

Roast Plums with Yogurt and Granola

Baked plums take on a complex, sweet flavor, and tart yogurt offers the perfect balance to this simple yet elegant dessert.

½ cup unsalted butter

1 cup packed light brown sugar

½ teaspoon ground star anise or cinnamon

1 teaspoon vanilla extract

¼ cup Mavrodaphne wine, port wine, or other fortified wine

8 medium-sized firm plums, pitted and halved

3 cups plain low-fat Greek yogurt

½ cup granola

SERVES 8

Per Serving:	
Calories	350
Fat	15g
Sodium	41mg
Carbohydrates	43g
Fiber	2g
Sugar	39g
Protein	10g

1 Preheat oven to 400°F.

2 Melt butter in a medium oven-safe skillet over medium heat. Stir in sugar, star anise, vanilla, and wine. Reduce heat to low and simmer for 5 minutes.

3 Place plums in the skillet cut side up. Spoon sauce over plums.

4 Bake plums in oven for 10–15 minutes until they are fork-tender but slightly firm. Set aside to cool for 10 minutes.

5 To serve, place 2 plum halves in a shallow bowl and top with yogurt and granola.

Chocolate Salami with Halva and Hazelnuts

Many tavernas in Greece will bring out a complementary small dessert after the meal. One such dessert is this mosaic of chocolate, halva, and nuts shaped like a salami. Dried fruit adds a tart component to the dessert, pulling back the sweetness just a bit.

2 cups semisweet chocolate chips

½ cup cocoa powder

1 cup tahini

1½ tablespoons grated orange zest

1 cup whole roasted hazelnuts

1 cup dried cherries or cranberries

1 cup chopped sesame halva

1 cup petit beurre cookies, broken into small pieces

2 tablespoons confectioners' sugar

1 Place chocolate chips in a large microwave-safe bowl and microwave on high in 30-second increments until almost completely melted. Stir with a spatula until all chips are melted.

2 Stir in cocoa powder, tahini, and orange zest. Add hazelnuts and cherries and stir until combined. Gently stir in halva and cookie pieces until evenly distributed.

3 Transfer mixture to a sheet of parchment paper. Use the paper to form the mixture into a long tube. Tightly twist the ends of the parchment and refrigerate for at least 3 hours.

4 Unwrap chilled salami carefully. Tie with butcher's twine (to resemble a whole salami) and place on a long platter. Dust with sugar before serving.

SERVES 12

Per Serving:

Calories	443
Fat	30g
Sodium	56mg
Carbohydrates	43g
Fiber	6g
Sugar	27g
Protein	8g

PETIT BEURRE BISCUITS

Petit beurre biscuits (cookies) can be found in the international section of the grocery store—look for LU brand from France. If you can't find them, you can substitute Nabisco Social Tea Biscuits.

Apricot and Walnut Tart

SERVES 6

Per Serving:

Calories	445
Fat	27g
Sodium	9mg
Carbohydrates	46g
Fiber	4g
Sugar	22g
Protein	9g

Any type of jam can be used in this recipe. Also, try other kinds of nuts, such as almonds or pecans, to create different flavors.

1 cup all-purpose flour

2 teaspoons olive oil

1 teaspoon ice water

2 cups chopped apricots

½ cup chopped walnuts

½ cup red currants

¼ cup apricot jam

¼ cup packed light brown sugar

1 Preheat oven to 375°F.

2 In a medium bowl, mix flour, oil, and water to form dough. On a floured surface, roll out dough into a 10" square and place on a baking sheet sprayed with nonstick cooking spray.

3 Arrange apricots, walnuts, currants, jam, and sugar in the center of the dough and fold edges together over filling to within 2" of the center. Fold back corners to leave an opening in center. Bake for 30 minutes.

Pear Croustade

A croustade is a French tart. Sweet, ripe pears are tossed in a lightly spiced mixture and baked atop a homemade crust. The aromas coming from your oven will make you swoon.

1½ cups plus 1 tablespoon all-purpose flour, divided

7 tablespoons sugar, divided

⅛ teaspoon salt

6 tablespoons cold unsalted butter, cut into ½" pieces

1 large egg yolk

6 tablespoons plain low-fat Greek yogurt

2 large, firm but ripe Bosc or Anjou pears, peeled, cored, and cut into thin wedges

1 tablespoon lemon juice

1 teaspoon anise seeds

⅓ teaspoon ground allspice

1 large egg white, lightly beaten

SERVES 8

Per Serving:

Calories	252
Fat	9g
Sodium	49mg
Carbohydrates	39g
Fiber	2g
Sugar	17g
Protein	4g

1 Place 1½ cups flour, 3 tablespoons sugar, and salt in a food processor. Add butter and pulse until mixture resembles coarse crumbs. Add egg yolk and pulse 2–3 times. Add yogurt 1 tablespoon at a time and pulse until absorbed.

2 Transfer dough to a floured work surface and form it into a flat disc. Wrap dough in plastic wrap and refrigerate for 30 minutes.

3 Preheat oven to 400°F. Line a large baking sheet with parchment paper.

4 Roll out dough on floured parchment to a 12" round. Transfer to prepared baking sheet.

5 In a large bowl, toss pears with 3 tablespoons sugar, remaining 1 tablespoon flour, lemon juice, anise, and allspice. Spread pear mixture on the center of the dough circle, leaving a 2" border.

6 Fold the edges of the dough over the outside edges of the fruit to create a rim (the center of the pears will be uncovered), crimping slightly as you go. Brush dough with egg white and sprinkle with remaining 1 tablespoon sugar.

7 Bake for 40 minutes or until crust is golden and filling is bubbling. Cool for 15 minutes.

8 Slide a large metal spatula under the crust and transfer to a large plate. Serve warm or at room temperature.

PAIR PEARS WITH SPICES

Pull this recipe out when pears are in season. The crust is very easy to prepare and the slight anise accent goes so well with pears. Another spice that works well with pears is some ground cardamom.

Apple Tart

SERVES 8

Per Serving:

Calories	447
Fat	24g
Sodium	89mg
Carbohydrates	57g
Fiber	4g
Sugar	35g
Protein	3g

COMMERCIAL PUFF PASTRY

In the past, puff pastry was made only in bakeries and sometimes sold to customers for their own baking needs. Soon, adventurous home bakers would try their hand at making their own puff pastry. After realizing that making it at home was time consuming, food companies saw a niche and began to make and sell puff pastry. Most frozen varieties are quite good. Check the label to ensure that real butter is used in the product you are buying.

Firm apples like the Granny Smith variety are ideal for tarts because they hold up well in the heat of the oven. A puff pastry tart like this is so easy to make, but it will wow your guests.

1 sheet thawed frozen puff pastry

4 large Granny Smith apples, peeled, cored, and thinly sliced

¼ cup granulated sugar

¼ cup packed light brown sugar

1 teaspoon ground cinnamon

½ cup unsalted butter, cut into small pieces

½ cup apricot jam

2 tablespoons brandy

1 Preheat oven to 400°F. Line a large baking sheet with parchment paper.

2 Place puff pastry on prepared baking sheet. Place a row of overlapping apple slices diagonally down the middle. Continue to make diagonal overlapping rows on both sides of the middle row.

3 Sprinkle with granulated sugar, brown sugar, and cinnamon. Dot apple slices with butter pieces.

4 Bake for 50–60 minutes until pastry is golden brown and apples are fork-tender and golden.

5 Melt jam in a small saucepan over medium heat. Remove from heat and stir in brandy.

6 Brush jam mixture over apples while still warm. Set aside to cool for at least 20 minutes before serving.

Date Almond Pie

For an added kick, use honey-flavored Greek yogurt in this tart. If you have a favorite dough recipe, you can make this in the shape of a free-form tart instead of using a pie shell. Spread the dough on a large baking sheet, top with the date mixture, and fold in the edges before baking.

1 cup chopped dried dates

½ cup chopped almonds

½ cup honey

1 (9") unbaked pie shell

1 cup plain nonfat Greek yogurt

¼ cup confectioners' sugar

1 Preheat oven to 375°F.

2 Mix dates, almonds, and honey in a medium bowl. Pour mixture into pie shell.

3 Bake for 20 minutes. Cool and serve with a dollop of yogurt and a sprinkle of sugar.

SERVES 6	
Per Serving:	
Calories	371
Fat	11g
Sodium	135mg
Carbohydrates	64g
Fiber	4g
Sugar	46g
Protein	8g

Pasteli (Honey Sesame Bars)

MAKES 20 PIECES

Per Serving (1 piece):

Calories	152
Fat	6g
Sodium	5mg
Carbohydrates	24g
Fiber	2g
Sugar	21g
Protein	2g

These delicious sesame bars contain healthy fats, protein, fiber, and antioxidants—they're the original energy snack. Choose a good-quality honey for these bars.

1½ **cups honey**

1½ **cups toasted sesame seeds**

½ **cup roughly chopped roasted unsalted almonds**

1 **tablespoon grated orange zest**

¼ **teaspoon ground cinnamon**

1 Line an unrimmed cookie sheet with parchment paper and set aside.

2 Pour honey into a medium saucepan and clip a candy thermometer to the side of the pan. Heat over medium heat until temperature reaches 250°F.

3 Add sesame seeds, almonds, orange zest, and cinnamon. Cook and stir for 3 minutes.

4 Pour mixture onto prepared cookie sheet and lay another piece of parchment paper on top.

5 Use a rolling pin to roll out mixture to ¼" thickness. Remove the top sheet of parchment and allow about 30 minutes to cool completely.

6 Cut into square or diamond shapes and serve. Store in an airtight container with parchment paper placed between layers for up to 1 week.

Apple Crisp

Per Serving:

Calories	307
Fat	12g
Sodium	83mg
Carbohydrates	49g
Fiber	3g
Sugar	33g
Protein	2g

Although not a traditional Mediterranean dish, the cinnamon in apple crisp speaks to a Mediterranean palate. It's easy to make, tastes great, and keeps well in the refrigerator for a few days. Warm up leftover crisp and serve it with a scoop of vanilla ice cream.

4 cups sliced tart apples

¾ cup all-purpose flour

1 cup packed light brown sugar

1 teaspoon ground cinnamon

¼ teaspoon salt

½ cup cold unsalted butter, cut into 8 pieces

½ cup rolled oats

1 Preheat oven to 350°F. Butter an 8" square baking dish.

2 Place apples in prepared dish.

3 In a medium bowl, mix flour, sugar, cinnamon, and salt. Cut in butter with a pastry cutter or a large fork. Stir in oats. Spread mixture evenly over apples.

4 Bake for 35–45 minutes until apples are tender.

5 Serve warm or at room temperature.

Cherry Clafouti

This easy French dessert features sweet ripe cherries baked in a custard mixture. Serve it with a scoop of French vanilla ice cream.

2 cups pitted sweet cherries

1 cup whole milk

2 large eggs

3 tablespoons all-purpose flour

3 tablespoons granulated sugar

1 teaspoon vanilla extract

¼ teaspoon almond extract

⅛ teaspoon sea salt

3 tablespoons confectioners' sugar

SERVES 8	
Per Serving:	
Calories	102
Fat	2g
Sodium	67mg
Carbohydrates	18g
Fiber	1g
Sugar	14g
Protein	3g

1 Preheat oven to 375°F.
2 Place cherries in a 9" round pie plate.
3 In a medium bowl, combine milk, eggs, flour, granulated sugar, vanilla and almond extracts, and salt. Beat with a whisk until smooth. Pour mixture over cherries.
4 Bake for 30 minutes or until the top is puffed up and golden.
5 Allow to cool for 15 minutes. Dust with confectioners' sugar before serving.

Fruit-Stuffed French Toast

The rich, eggy flavor of challah is perfect for this easy special-occasion French toast.

SERVES 12

Per Serving:

Calories	170
Fat	3g
Sodium	156mg
Carbohydrates	30g
Fiber	1g
Sugar	12g
Protein	6g

EASY BREAKFAST FOR A CROWD

Baked French toast is perfect for the times you have a houseful of overnight guests. Prepare all your ingredients, assemble them in a baking dish, and pop it in the oven. You'll have a stress-free breakfast, allowing you time to mix some mimosas for your guests (and yourself!).

½ teaspoon olive oil

1 large loaf challah bread, sliced into 6 (3"-thick) slices

½ cup sliced strawberries

½ cup blueberries

1 cup diced peaches

2 large eggs

4 large egg whites

¼ cup skim milk

¼ cup plain nonfat Greek yogurt

½ cup orange marmalade or apricot jam

¼ cup confectioners' sugar

1 Preheat oven to 375°F. Grease a large baking dish with oil.

2 Cut a slit into the bottom crust of each bread slice to form a pocket.

3 Mix strawberries, blueberries, and peaches in a medium bowl. Fill each bread pocket with about ⅓ cup fruit mixture. Press pocket closed.

4 In a large, shallow bowl, beat eggs, egg whites, and milk. Dip bread into egg mixture, letting it fully absorb the mixture. Place bread in prepared baking dish. Bake for 20 minutes, flipping bread halfway through.

5 Remove French toast from oven and cut each slice in half diagonally. Serve each half with dollop of yogurt, a spoonful of marmalade or jam, and a sprinkling of sugar.

Olive Oil Cake with Mixed Fruit

A mild, fruity olive oil works for this recipe. The marketplace has a wide array of olive oils from the Mediterranean, California, and even Australia! Choose the olive oil that tastes best to you.

1¼ cups granulated sugar

2 large eggs

½ cup whole milk

½ cup olive oil

2 teaspoons vanilla extract

1½ cups all-purpose flour

2½ teaspoons baking powder

⅛ teaspoon salt

1 cup sliced strawberries

1 cup pineapple tidbits

1½ tablespoons grated orange zest

¼ cup confectioners' sugar

1. Preheat oven to 375°F. Line a 9" × 5" loaf pan with parchment paper.
2. Place granulated sugar, eggs, milk, oil, and vanilla in a medium bowl. Use a hand mixer to beat for 5 minutes.
3. Place flour, baking powder, and salt in a small bowl and mix with a fork. Add to egg mixture and stir with a spatula until incorporated. Fold in strawberries, pineapple, and orange zest.
4. Pour batter into prepared pan. Bake for 50–55 minutes until a toothpick inserted in the center comes out clean.
5. Cool in pan for 5 minutes. Remove from pan and cool on a wire rack for 30 minutes.
6. Transfer to a platter and top with a dusting of confectioners' sugar before serving.

SERVES 8

Per Serving:

Calories	389
Fat	16g
Sodium	176mg
Carbohydrates	59g
Fiber	1g
Sugar	39g
Protein	5g

DON'T CALL IT A FRUITCAKE

This is not the old-fashioned, brick-like Christmas fruitcake! This fruity and slightly dense cake will remind you more of a trifle spiked with fruit. Mix up the berries if you like, but be sure to include the pineapple. It's the secret ingredient for a moist cake.

Sicilian Whole Orange Cake

Versions of this cake can be found in both Italy and Greece. If you love citrus, this is the cake for you! Garnish with orange slices.

2 medium unpeeled oranges, boiled for 10 minutes in water to cover, then drained

6 large eggs

1¼ cups sugar

1 cup light olive oil

2 teaspoons vanilla extract

2 cups all-purpose flour

3 teaspoons baking powder

SERVES 12

Per Serving:

Calories	365
Fat	21g
Sodium	127mg
Carbohydrates	40g
Fiber	1g
Sugar	23g
Protein	5g

1 Preheat oven to 375°F. Grease a 9" cake pan.

2 Place boiled oranges in a food processor and pulse until puréed.

3 In a large bowl, whisk together eggs, sugar, oil, and vanilla until smooth. Stir in orange purée.

4 In a small bowl, add flour and baking powder and stir with a fork. Add to orange mixture and stir with a spatula until incorporated.

5 Pour batter into prepared pan. Bake for 45–50 minutes until a toothpick inserted in the center comes out clean.

6 Cool in pan for 5 minutes. Remove from pan and cool on a wire rack for 30 minutes before serving.

GLUTEN-FREE ORANGE CAKE

This cake can be made gluten-free by replacing the all-purpose flour with ground almond flour. The orange and almond flavors complement each other so well, you might want to try it even if you're not looking for a gluten-free cake.

Corn Bread with Greek Yogurt and Chocolate Chips

SERVES 8

Per Serving:

Calories	483
Fat	23g
Sodium	123mg
Carbohydrates	62g
Fiber	2g
Sugar	32g
Protein	8g

Corn bread is naturally sweet, with a wonderful yellow color. If you wish, you can replace the sugar with an equal amount of honey.

1 cup fine cornmeal

1 cup all-purpose flour

2 teaspoons baking powder

¾ cup granulated sugar

⅔ cup vegetable oil

2 large eggs

2 tablespoons orange marmalade

2 teaspoons vanilla extract

1 cup plain low-fat Greek yogurt

½ cup semisweet chocolate chips

¼ cup confectioners' sugar

1 Preheat oven to 375°F. Line a 9" × 5" loaf pan with parchment paper.

2 Place cornmeal, flour, and baking powder in a medium bowl and mix with a fork. Set aside.

3 Place granulated sugar, oil, eggs, marmalade, and vanilla in a large bowl. Use a hand mixer to beat for 5 minutes. Stir in cornmeal mixture. Add yogurt and chocolate chips and fold in with a spatula.

4 Pour batter into prepared pan. Bake for 50–55 minutes until a toothpick inserted in the center comes out clean.

5 Cool in pan for 5 minutes. Remove from pan and cool on a wire rack for 30 minutes.

6 Transfer to a platter and top with a dusting of confectioners' sugar before serving.

Lenten Cake

In the Mediterranean region, cakes that don't include dairy or eggs are often served during Lent. But this vegan cake is good any time of the year. If you have rose water, add a tablespoon with the ouzo. It will add a lightly floral scent and flavor.

3½ cups all-purpose flour

½ teaspoon salt

½ cup ground almonds

1 teaspoon baking powder

1 tablespoon ground cinnamon

¼ teaspoon ground cloves

2 tablespoons grated orange zest

1 tablespoon grated lemon zest

1½ cups orange juice

1 teaspoon baking soda

1 cup granulated sugar

1 cup extra-virgin olive oil

1 ounce ouzo or brandy

¼ cup chopped walnuts

¼ cup dried cranberries

¼ cup chopped dried cherries

¼ cup raisins

¼ cup toasted sesame seeds

2 tablespoons confectioners' sugar

SERVES 12

Per Serving:

Calories	303
Fat	5g
Sodium	236mg
Carbohydrates	59g
Fiber	3g
Sugar	26g
Protein	6g

1 Preheat oven to 350°F. Grease and flour a Bundt pan.

2 In a large bowl, place flour, salt, almonds, baking powder, cinnamon, cloves, orange zest, and lemon zest and mix well.

3 In a small bowl, combine orange juice and baking soda. Pour into flour mixture along with granulated sugar, oil, and ouzo. Stir until just combined. Fold in walnuts, cranberries, cherries, raisins, and sesame seeds.

4 Pour batter into prepared pan and bake for 45 minutes until a toothpick inserted in the center comes out clean.

5 Cool in the pan for 5 minutes, then carefully invert the cake onto a wire rack. Set aside until completely cool, at least 1 hour.

6 Transfer to a cake plate and dust with confectioners' sugar.

Rizogalo

This rice pudding is particularly good when refrigerated for a few hours and served on warm, sunny days. The citrus zest adds a whole new dimension of flavor to the dish.

SERVES 8

Per Serving:

Calories	385
Fat	9g
Sodium	111mg
Carbohydrates	66g
Fiber	1g
Sugar	50g
Protein	10g

ARBORIO

Arborio rice is a short-grain rice with a creamy texture. Most supermarkets now carry Arborio rice as well as a number of other varieties.

8¼ cups cold whole milk, divided

1 cup Arborio rice

1½ cups sugar

1 teaspoon vanilla extract

1 tablespoon finely shredded citrus zest (orange, lemon, or lime)

2 large egg yolks

1 tablespoon corn flour

1 teaspoon ground cinnamon

1 In a large saucepan over medium-high heat, bring 8 cups milk to a slight boil. Add rice and stir well until mixture boils. Reduce heat to medium-low and gently simmer uncovered for 30 minutes, stirring regularly so milk doesn't stick to sides or bottom of the pan.

2 Add sugar, vanilla, and zest and continue to simmer. Stir occasionally for another 10 minutes.

3 Beat egg yolks with remaining ¼ cup milk; whisk in corn flour and mix well.

4 Pour egg yolk mixture into saucepan and whisk well to incorporate. Simmer for 3–5 minutes until thick.

5 Remove from heat. Transfer mixture into eight small bowls. Let stand for 1 hour to cool. Sprinkle with cinnamon. Refrigerate until cold or serve at room temperature.

Rice and Raisin Pudding

Rice pudding is a popular dessert in Mediterranean restaurants. It's a small bowl of comfort.

3 cups water

1 cup Arborio rice

4 cups warm whole milk

1 tablespoon unsalted butter

¾ cup sugar

⅛ teaspoon salt

3 (1") strips lemon peel

1 (2") cinnamon stick

2 teaspoons vanilla extract

¼ cup cornstarch

¼ cup cold whole milk

½ cup raisins

1 teaspoon ground cinnamon

SERVES 8	
Per Serving:	
Calories	280
Fat	6g
Sodium	97mg
Carbohydrates	52g
Fiber	1g
Sugar	31g
Protein	6g

1 Place water in a medium saucepan and bring to a boil over high heat, then add rice. When mixture returns to a boil, reduce heat to medium-low and cover saucepan. Simmer for 16–18 minutes until rice is tender.

2 Increase heat to medium and add warm milk, butter, sugar, salt, lemon peel, cinnamon stick, and vanilla. Bring to a boil, then reduce heat to low. Simmer, stirring constantly, for 10 minutes.

3 In a small bowl, mix cornstarch and cold milk. Stir cornstarch mixture into rice mixture. Add raisins and simmer for 5 minutes.

4 Remove and discard lemon peel and cinnamon stick. Pour pudding into eight small bowls. Sprinkle with ground cinnamon.

5 Serve warm or refrigerate for at least 2 hours.

Apple and Brown Rice Pudding

SERVES 6

Per Serving:

Calories	234
Fat	2g
Sodium	66mg
Carbohydrates	52g
Fiber	3g
Sugar	23g
Protein	4g

This rice pudding is perfect to eat on crisp fall days. The brown rice adds extra fiber, and the raisins contribute a rich caramel sweetness. If you are making this for vegans, replace the honey with maple syrup.

2 cups almond milk

1 cup long-grain brown rice

½ cup golden raisins

1 medium Granny Smith apple, peeled, cored, and chopped

¼ cup honey

1 teaspoon vanilla extract

½ teaspoon ground cinnamon

1 Place all ingredients in the Instant Pot®. Stir to combine. Close lid, press the Manual or Pressure Cook button, and adjust time to 20 minutes.

2 When the timer beeps, let pressure release naturally for 15 minutes, then quick-release the remaining pressure. Press the Cancel button and open lid. Serve warm or at room temperature.

Semolina Halva with Ice Cream Surprise

This version of halva is made with semolina flour, which looks similar to Cream of Wheat. In fact, you can use Cream of Wheat if you can't find coarse semolina flour. The scoop of ice cream in the middle makes for a pleasant surprise when you cut into it.

½ cup unsalted butter

1 cup coarse semolina flour

¼ cup pine nuts

1 cup sugar

2 cups cold water

2 whole cloves

1 (1") cinnamon stick

1 cup vanilla ice cream

½ teaspoon ground cinnamon

SERVES 4

Per Serving:

Calories	618
Fat	27g
Sodium	34mg
Carbohydrates	89g
Fiber	2g
Sugar	58g
Protein	7g

1 Melt butter in a medium saucepan over medium heat. Add semolina and pine nuts. Cook, stirring, for 10–12 minutes until semolina is toasted and deep golden in color.

2 Stir in sugar, water, cloves, and cinnamon stick. Cook, stirring constantly, for 10 minutes or until all liquid is absorbed and mixture forms a porridge consistency.

3 Remove from heat. Remove and discard cloves and cinnamon stick. Cover pan with a clean kitchen towel and top with lid. Set aside for 5 minutes.

4 Divide mixture into eight equal portions. Use a spoon to press one portion into the bottom and sides of a ramekin or small bowl. Scoop ¼ cup ice cream onto the halva shell, then top with a second portion of halva. Spread halva to the edges of ramekin so ice cream is sealed inside.

5 Place a small plate on top of the ramekin and quickly insert the ice cream–filled halva onto the plate. Lift and remove the ramekin. Repeat with remaining halva and ice cream.

6 Sprinkle with ground cinnamon and serve immediately.

Tahini and Honey Ice Cream

Tahini is made from ground sesame seeds and is full of healthy fats, nutrients, and vitamins. It is also a great substitute for peanut butter.

SERVES 8

Per Serving:

Calories	340
Fat	18g
Sodium	59mg
Carbohydrates	42g
Fiber	2g
Sugar	35g
Protein	6g

2 cups unsweetened almond milk

1 tablespoon vanilla extract

1 cup tahini

½ cup confectioners' sugar

1 ounce amaretto liqueur

¾ cup honey, divided

2 tablespoons sesame seeds

AMARETTO ANTIFREEZE

Adding a small amount of alcohol to the ice cream means it will not freeze into a solid block. And amaretto adds a lovely almond flavor to this frozen treat.

1 Place the bowl of an ice cream maker in the freezer.
2 Place milk, vanilla, tahini, sugar, amaretto, and ½ cup honey in a medium bowl. Stir to combine, then cover and refrigerate for at least 4 hours.
3 Pour the chilled mixture into an ice cream maker and continue according to the manufacturer's directions. Scrape mixture into a covered plastic container and freeze for at least 2 hours.
4 Scoop ice cream into eight bowls and drizzle with remaining ¼ cup honey. Sprinkle with sesame seeds and serve immediately.

No-Churn Ice Cream with Turkish Delight

SERVES 6

Per Serving:

Calories	606
Fat	37g
Sodium	114mg
Carbohydrates	59g
Fiber	1g
Sugar	56g
Protein	9g

TURKISH DELIGHT

Turkish Delight candies are similar in texture to Jujubes, and they come in many different flavors and colors. Look for Turkish or Greek Delight at Middle Eastern or Greek shops or online.

You can make ice cream without an ice cream maker! This method requires a stand mixer or a hand mixer and a bowl. The key is to whip the cream, add the flavor base, and simply freeze.

2 cups cold heavy cream

1 (14-ounce) can sweetened condensed milk

3 tablespoons rose water

3 tablespoons vodka

2 drops red liquid food coloring

1 cup finely chopped rosewater-flavored Turkish Delight

¼ cup chopped pistachios

1 In the bowl of a stand mixer, add cream and condensed milk. Use the whisk attachment to beat on high speed until soft peaks form.
2 Reduce speed to medium and add rose water, vodka, food coloring, and Turkish Delight. Beat for 2–3 minutes until well incorporated.
3 Transfer to a rectangular plastic container and smooth the top. Place a piece of plastic wrap directly on the surface and cover with the container lid. Freeze for at least 5 hours or overnight.
4 Serve with a garnish of chopped pistachios.

Cantaloupe Granita

In the summer, cantaloupe melons are easy to find anywhere you shop. Bring home an extra melon or two to make this easy and refreshing granita.

2 cups cubed cantaloupe
¼ cup sugar
2 teaspoons lemon juice
¼ cup chopped fresh mint

1 Place all ingredients in a blender and purée until smooth.
2 Pour into a 13" × 9" metal baking pan and freeze for 1 hour until mixture forms a slushy consistency.
3 Scrape granita with a fork and scoop into chilled martini glasses or small dessert bowls. Serve immediately.

SERVES 4

Per Serving:

Calories	78
Fat	0g
Sodium	13mg
Carbohydrates	20g
Fiber	1g
Sugar	18g
Protein	1g

CANTALOUPE NUTRITION

One serving of cantaloupe will provide you with 100 percent of your daily requirement for both vitamins A and C. It's also a good source of potassium. And at only 53 calories per cup, it's an appealing and healthful snack.

STANDARD US/METRIC
MEASUREMENT CONVERSIONS

VOLUME CONVERSIONS

US Volume Measure	Metric Equivalent
⅛ teaspoon	0.5 milliliter
¼ teaspoon	1 milliliter
½ teaspoon	2 milliliters
1 teaspoon	5 milliliters
½ tablespoon	7 milliliters
1 tablespoon (3 teaspoons)	15 milliliters
2 tablespoons (1 fluid ounce)	30 milliliters
¼ cup (4 tablespoons)	60 milliliters
⅓ cup	90 milliliters
½ cup (4 fluid ounces)	125 milliliters
⅔ cup	160 milliliters
¾ cup (6 fluid ounces)	180 milliliters
1 cup (16 tablespoons)	250 milliliters
1 pint (2 cups)	500 milliliters
1 quart (4 cups)	1 liter (about)

WEIGHT CONVERSIONS

US Weight Measure	Metric Equivalent
½ ounce	15 grams
1 ounce	30 grams
2 ounces	60 grams
3 ounces	85 grams
¼ pound (4 ounces)	115 grams
½ pound (8 ounces)	225 grams
¾ pound (12 ounces)	340 grams
1 pound (16 ounces)	454 grams

OVEN TEMPERATURE CONVERSIONS

Degrees Fahrenheit	Degrees Celsius
200 degrees F	95 degrees C
250 degrees F	120 degrees C
275 degrees F	135 degrees C
300 degrees F	150 degrees C
325 degrees F	160 degrees C
350 degrees F	180 degrees C
375 degrees F	190 degrees C
400 degrees F	205 degrees C
425 degrees F	220 degrees C
450 degrees F	230 degrees C

BAKING PAN SIZES

American	Metric
8 × 1½ inch round baking pan	20 × 4 cm cake tin
9 × 1½ inch round baking pan	23 × 3.5 cm cake tin
11 × 7 × 1½ inch baking pan	28 × 18 × 4 cm baking tin
13 × 9 × 2 inch baking pan	30 × 20 × 5 cm baking tin
2 quart rectangular baking dish	30 × 20 × 3 cm baking tin
15 × 10 × 2 inch baking pan	30 × 25 × 2 cm baking tin (Swiss roll tin)
9 inch pie plate	22 × 4 or 23 × 4 cm pie plate
7 or 8 inch springform pan	18 or 20 cm springform or loose bottom cake tin
9 × 5 × 3 inch loaf pan	23 × 13 × 7 cm or 2 lb narrow loaf or pate tin
1½ quart casserole	1.5 liter casserole
2 quart casserole	2 liter casserole

Index

300 EASY, HEALTHY MEDITERRANEAN RECIPES

for the Most Popular Kitchen Appliance— the Instant Pot®!

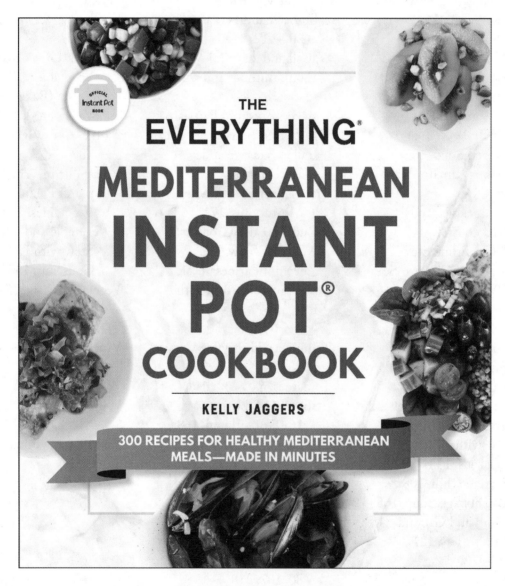

OFFICIAL Instant Pot BOOK

THE

EVERYTHING®

MEDITERRANEAN

INSTANT POT® COOKBOOK

KELLY JAGGERS

300 RECIPES FOR HEALTHY MEDITERRANEAN MEALS—MADE IN MINUTES

Pick Up or Download Your Copy Today!

adamsmedia
An Imprint of Simon & Schuster
A Paramount Company